FIFTH REVISED EDITION

PLAIN ENGLISH HANDBOOK

A Complete Guide to Good English

by **J. MARTYN WALSH**
and **ANNA KATHLEEN WALSH**

 McCORMICK-MATHERS PUBLISHING COMPANY, INC.

Wichita, Kansas 67201

PREFACE

This is a complete handbook containing all rules, definitions, and illustrations necessary to the mastery of functional grammar and usage.

The treatment of grammar given here is entirely descriptive. It is based on the most authoritative studies of the language actually in use in America, and not on anyone's opinion of what the language should be. Naturally, in view of the scope and purpose of this handbook, the usage presented is descriptive of literate written usage, except as otherwise labeled for the problems of informal spoken expression are usually not so critical as those of written expression and, furthermore, are too varied and complex to be contained in a single volume. Insofar as informal discourse should be natural, it is not a subject of instruction. The levels of usage are, of course, clearly explained in this book.

For the more advanced student some indications of the newer developments in language study are given in Chapter 8, "Structural and Transformational Grammars," Sections 579 to 629.

The sections are numbered, consecutively in bold figures throughout the book.

CONTENTS

One: SENTENCE COMPLETENESS

THE SENTENCE AND ITS PARTS

1 A **sentence** is a word or a group of words expressing a complete thought. It should begin with a capital letter:

The book is on the table.

2 A sentence must have a **subject** and a **predicate**, either expressed or understood, and it may have an object or other complement, modifiers, connectives, and independent elements.

3 The **subject** is that of which something is said:

Flowers bloom.   *Shakespeare* wrote plays.
Squirrels climb trees.   *Denver* is in Colorado.

4 The **predicate** is that which is said of the subject:

Flowers *bloom*.   Shakespeare *wrote plays*.
Squirrels *climb trees*.   Denver *is in Colorado*.

Diagram—Sentence with *simple subject* (13)* and *simple predicate* (15):
Fish swim.

Fish	swim

5 Although a sentence must have a subject and a predicate in order to be grammatically complete, in an elliptical sentence (a sentence from which a word or words are properly omitted) either the subject or the predicate or both may be unexpressed:

Subject omitted: *(You)* Read this story.
Predicate omitted: Who spoke? John *(spoke)*.
Subject and predicate omitted: What did I bring? *(I brought)* Books.

6 The receiver of the action denoted by the simple predicate is the **direct object** (sometimes called the **object complement**):

The carpenter built a *house*.
The girls gathered *flowers*.

Diagram—Sentence with *direct object* of a verb:
Farmers grow *wheat*.

Farmers	grow	wheat

The direct object may be **compound** (17):

We saw *rocks* and *trees*.

*Numbers in parentheses refer to sections of this book.

1

Diagram—Sentence with *compound direct object* of verb:

Dad planted *shrubs* and *flowers.*

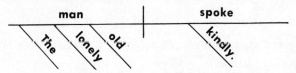

7 A **modifier** is a word or a group of words that changes the meaning of another word:

She sang *beautifully.* (*Beautifully* modifies *sang.*)
The *little old* man laughed. (*The, little,* and *old* modify *man.*)
The boy *at the desk* is Fred. (*At the desk* modifies *boy.*)
The girl *whom you saw* is Jane. (*Whom you saw* modifies *girl.*)

Diagram—Sentence with *modifiers* of subject and predicate:

The *lonely old* man spoke *kindly.*

8 A group of related words not having a subject and a predicate is called a **phrase:**

The book *on the desk* is a grammar.

9 A group of related words having a subject and a predicate and used as part of a sentence is called a **clause:**

Mary is the girl *who sang.* (Subject is *who;* predicate is *sang.*)

10 Although a sentence or a clause must have a subject and a predicate, either can be correct with only one word expressed:

Go. (sentence)
The coach said, *"Go."* (clause)

In both the sentence and the clause above, the omitted subject *you* is clearly understood.

11 **Connectives** merely join parts of the sentence:

Girls *and* boys play tennis. (conjunction, 43)
He came *with* me. (preposition, 42)

12 **Independent elements** are expressions that have no grammatical connection with the sentence in which they are found. They are of several kinds:

1. **Interjection:** *Hurrah!* We won.
2. **Direct address:** *Ruth,* I want you to help me.

3. **Exclamation:** *Poor girl!* She needs our help.
4. **Parenthetical expression:** He went, *I am sure,* to please us.
5. **Responsive:** *No,* he has not come.
6. **Nominative absolute:** *The work being done,* we went home.

Note: Most independent elements are set off from the rest of the sentence by commas (479); however the interjection and exclamation are set off by exclamation marks.

13 The **simple subject** is the subject taken without any modifier (7):
The little bird sang gaily.

The simple subject may consist of more than one word:
Betty Ruth Mills is a singer.

14 The **complete subject** is the simple subject with all its modifiers:
The little bird sang gaily.
The girl at the piano is Evelyn.

15 The **simple predicate** is the predicate taken without any modifier or complement. The simple predicate may consist of more than one word, for it may include a main verb and its helpers (a verb phrase, 39):
The girl *has tried* patiently.
The book *should have been returned.*

16 The **complete predicate** is the predicate with all its complements and modifiers:
The girl *has tried patiently.*
The boy *went swiftly from the room.*

17 A **compound subject** is one made up of two or more simple subjects:
Flowers and *trees* are beautiful.

18 A **compound predicate** consists of two or more simple predicates:
Healthy boys *work* and *play.*

19 Both the subject and predicate may be compound:
Girls and *boys study* and *play.*

Diagram—Sentence with *compound subject* and *compound predicate:*
Boys and *girls play* and *sing.*

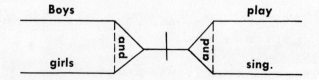

CLASSIFICATION OF SENTENCES

20 Sentences are classified according to their structure, or form, as **simple, compound,** and **complex.** (A less common type, the **compound-complex,** is described in section 402.)

21 A **simple sentence** has but **one** independent clause (386) and **no** dependent clause (387):

> Our team won the game.

The subject and predicate of a simple sentence may both be compound (19):

> Mary and Ruth played and sang at the party. (A simple sentence may have any number of phrases—*at the party* is a phrase—but it cannot contain a dependent clause.)

22 A **compound sentence** is equivalent to two or more simple sentences (called **independent clauses** when used as a single sentence) connected by a word, by words, or by punctuation:

> Joe does good work and he will succeed.
>
> Joo does good work; he will succeed.
>
> Joe does good work. He will succeed. (**two simple sentences**)

(Notice the three ways of writing these words. The last way is not a compound sentence; it is two simple sentences.)

23 A **complex sentence** is one that contains but **one** independent clause (386) and **one or more** dependent clauses (387):

> I was not at home when he came. (The clause *when he came* is dependent.)

Note: Although the definition for the complex sentence given above is the conventional one, there is a type of complex sentence in which the independent clause is not apparent. In this type a noun clause may be an essential element of the independent clause:

> *That she is intelligent* is obvious. (**subject**)
>
> The truth is *that he forgot.* (**predicate nominative**)
>
> She said *that she would accept the offer.* (**object**)

24 As to use, sentences are divided into four classes: **declarative, imperative, interrogative,** and **exclamatory.**

25 A **declarative sentence** makes a statement:

> Our glee club sings well.

26 The **imperative sentence** expresses a command or an entreaty:

> Do not walk on the grass. (The subject of an imperative sentence is *you;* it is usually omitted.)

27 The **interrogative sentence** asks a question:

> Where shall we go?

28 The **exclamatory sentence** expresses surprise or strong emotion:
How beautiful the sunset is!

A declarative, an interrogative, or an imperative sentence may also be exclamatory if expressed excitedly; therefore some grammarians do not list the exclamatory sentence as a separate class.

28A The **natural order** of the sentence is for the subject to precede the predicate:
George went to school.

28B When the complete predicate or a part of it precedes the subject, the sentence is in **inverted order:**
To school went George.

In the interrogative sentence (27) and in a sentence beginning with expletive (232) *there* or the adverbs *there* or *here*, the predicate or a part of it usually precedes the subject:
Have you *received* the book?
There *are* three books on the desk.
Here *comes* Charlie.

29 **End Punctuation.** The punctuation at the end of sentences is very important. The declarative sentence (25) ends with a period. The imperative sentence (26) ends with a period. The interrogative sentence (27) closes with a question mark. The exclamatory sentence (28) usually ends with an exclamation mark:
The trees are most beautiful in autumn. (declarative)
Come to see me next Christmas. (imperative)
Do you like English? (interrogative)
How beautiful the roses are! (exclamatory)

30 **Capitalization.** Every sentence (except one in parentheses within another sentence) should begin with a capital letter. This is a very important rule.

WRITING GOOD SENTENCES

31 **Do not omit the subject from a declarative sentence:**
Incorrect: Saw you at the show last night. (declarative)
Correct: *I* saw you at the show last night.

(Subjects are properly omitted from imperative sentences, 26.)

32 **Do not write a fragment of a sentence as if it were complete:**
Incorrect: He studied hard. Hoping to win the prize. (The words *hoping to win the prize* form a phrase which modifies *he*.)
Correct: He studied hard, hoping to win the prize.

> **Incorrect:** Anne had a good time. While she was in the East last summer. (The words *while she was in the East last summer* form a dependent clause used as a modifier.)
>
> **Correct:** Anne had a good time while she was in the East last summer.

33 Do not write two or more sentences together as one, without punctuation:

> **Incorrect:** We started early we were eager for the trip.
>
> **Correct:** We started early. We were eager for the trip.
>
> **Correct:** We started early; we were eager for the trip.

34 Learn to distinguish a sentence from a fragment and from more than one sentence. The ability to distinguish between a sentence and a group of words which is more or less than a sentence is called **sentence sense.**

While we waited for the train. (This group of words, which resembles a dependent clause, is not a sentence; it is a fragment.)

Men and women running. (Because these words do not have a predicate, they do not form a sentence.)

They are running. (This group of words is a sentence. It expresses a complete thought and has both a subject and a predicate.)

Ask your teacher to help you. (This is an imperative sentence. The subject *you* is understood.)

Don plays football he is captain of the team. (Two sentences are incorrectly written as one. This can be corrected in three ways: 1. Don plays football. He is captain of the team. 2. Don plays football; he is captain of the team. 3. Don plays football, and he is captain of the team.)

That was a good game our boys played well were you there? (Three sentences are incorrectly written as one. This can be corrected: That was a good game. Our boys played well. Were you there?)

35 Do not splice sentences or independent clauses together with a comma:

> **Incorrect:** My brother studies French, he hopes to become a famous singer. (Two sentences are incorrectly written as one.)
>
> **Correct:** My brother studies French. He hopes to become a famous singer.

Two: THE PARTS OF SPEECH

DEFINITIONS

36 All words may be classified into eight groups called **parts of speech.** The group to which a word belongs is determined by its use in the sentence; therefore the same word may be any one of several parts of speech, depending upon its use in a given sentence. The eight parts of speech are **noun, pronoun, verb, adjective, adverb, preposition, conjunction,** and **interjection.**

37 A **noun** is a name of persons, places, things, ideas, or qualities.

Robert Frost wrote *poems.*   *Ann* lives in *Boston.*

Work brings *success.*   *People* like *admiration.*

38 A **pronoun** is a word used to take the place of a noun. Through its use, one may avoid repeating names:

Mary has lost *her* book.

Ruth saw the boys and talked with *them.*

39 A **verb** is a word used to express action, being, or state of being:

That man *is* a banker.

Helen *painted* a picture.

A verb may be composed of several words, called a **verb phrase:**

This book *should* have been *sent* to the library.

40 An **adjective** is used to modify a noun or a pronoun. An adjective may be a single word, a phrase, or a clause:

We saw *beautiful* valleys and *rugged* mountains. (**single words**)

The rug *on the floor* is blue. (**phrase**)

The man *who spoke* is a teacher. (**clause**)

41 An **adverb** is used to modify a verb, an adjective, or another adverb. It may be a single word, a phrase, or a clause:

She sang *beautifully.* (**single word**)

The stranger came *into the room.* (**phrase**)

Robert left *when I came.* (**clause**)

In some cases adverbs may modify other parts of speech   (307).*

42 A **preposition** shows the relation between its object and some other word in the sentence:

We walked *through* the woods. (*Through* shows the relation between *woods,* its object, and *walked,* the verb.)

* *Numbers in parentheses refer to sections of this book.*

7

43 A **conjunction** connects words or groups of words:

Bob *and* Nell are here.   She came *but* she did not stay.

44 An **interjection** expresses strong feeling: *Ouch! Oh!*

The interjection has no grammatical relation to the rest of the sentence.

45 A **substantive** is any word or group of words used as a noun (37) or as a noun equivalent (58).

46 **Inflection** is any change in the form of a word to indicate a change in its meaning: *book—books, I—me, has—have.*

I *have* sent the *book.*   He *has* sent the *books* to me.

47 The inflection of nouns and pronouns is called **declension** (139, 154): *man—men, he—him.*

He is a famous *man.*   The *men* are with *him.*

48 The inflection of adjectives and adverbs is called **comparison** (286): *small—smaller—smallest, fast—faster—fastest.*

The *small* boy ran fast, but the *smaller* boy ran faster.

49 The correct arrangement of the inflection of verbs is called **conjugation** (see 200).

50 The use of a word in a given sentence determines what part of speech it is; therefore, while a word may be one part of speech in a particular sentence, it may be used as a different part of speech in another sentence:

We saw a *rock fence.* (adjective, 40)
That *rock* is beautiful. (noun, 37)
You must not *rock* the boat. (verb, 39)
The word *but* may be almost any part of speech. (noun, 37)
We walked *but* a short distance. (adverb, 41)
All came *but* Ann. (preposition, 42)
We waited for him, *but* he did not come. (conjunction, 43)
They made five yards on the first *down.* (noun, 37)
Joe made a *down* payment on the car. (adjective, 40)
We walked *down* the hill. (preposition, 42)
The old house fell *down.* (adverb, 41)
Adversity will never *down* Bob. (verb, 39)

The following are a few of the great number of words that are commonly used as two or more parts of speech: *while, right, walk, rain, cry, play, paper, water, call, ground, land, stone, after, before, fast, outside, iron, last, paint, past, picnic, round, still, that, fly.*

NOUNS

51 There are two general classes of nouns: **proper** and **common.**

52 A **proper noun** is the name of a particular person, place, or thing; and it should be capitalized:

We are *Americans.*   *Jane* was born in *Alaska.*

53 A **common noun** is the name applied to a class or to any of a class of persons, places, or things:

The *man* walked down the *street.*   The *cow* is a domestic *animal.*

54 In addition to these general classes of nouns there are special classes: **abstract, concrete, collective, compound.**

Note: The **verbal noun,** though it is not in the strictest sense a pure noun, is very important. (See 58-4, 58-5, 195, 256-259.) It has some characteristics of both noun and verb, and it may be either an infinitive (194) or a gerund (195):

Writing business letters is important work. (*Writing* is a gerund, 195, used as subject of the sentence, but it retains verb force sufficiently to have *letters* as its object.)

To *write* good letters requires skill. (*To write* is an infinitive, 194, used as subject of the sentence; *letters* is the object of the infinitive.)

55 An **abstract noun** is a noun that names a quality or attribute:

We like *honesty* and *courtesy.*

Note: A noun that names something in a material form is called **concrete:**

A *rose* is on the *desk.*

56 A **collective noun** is a noun that names a group or collection (89, 233):

Our *school* has a strong football team.

57 A **compound noun** is a noun made up of two or more words. Some compounds are written as separate words, some are hyphenated, and others are written solid as one word: *fountain pen, father-in-law, maple sirup, secretary-general, have-not, businessman, newspaper, motorboat.*

The only safe guide in treating compounds is a dictionary.

Note: Some grammarians classify such nouns as *Duke of Wellington* and *editor in chief* as **phrasal nouns.**

58 There are many **noun equivalents** (substantives, 45), such as the following:

1. **Pronoun** (38): *She* is my teacher.
2. **Adjective** (40): The *young* are impatient.
3. **Adverb** (41): Since *then* I haven't seen him.

4. **Gerund** (195): *Walking* is good exercise.
5. **Infinitive** (194): *To win* is our intention.
6. **Phrase** (8): *Over the top* is our aim.
7. **Clause** (9, 385, 388): *That he has won* is a fact.
8. **Quotation** (394, 486): *"The time has arrived,"* the speaker said.

59 The **modifications** of nouns are **gender, person, number,** and **case.**

60 **Gender** is distinction as to sex; therefore there are properly but two classes of gender. However, the following four are given by many grammarians: **masculine, feminine, neuter, common.**

61 A noun which denotes a **male** is of the **masculine gender:** *man, boy, father, brother.*

62 A noun which denotes a **female** is of the **feminine gender:** *woman, girl, mother, sister.*

63 A noun which names an **object without sex** is of the **neuter gender:** *book, rock, desk, house.*

64 Nouns which denote **either males or females or both** are said to be of the **common gender:** *student, children, singers, teacher.*

65 There are three ways of indicating gender:
1. Gender may be indicated by a change of word: *man—woman, rooster—hen.*
2. Gender may be indicated by the addition of a word: *grandfather—grandmother, manservant—maidservant.*
3. Gender may be indicated by the use of suffixes: *host—hostess, hero—heroine.*

66 **Person** denotes the speaker, the person or thing spoken to, the person or thing spoken of. There are three classes: **first, second, third.**

Nouns used alone are always in the third person. When a noun is used in apposition to a pronoun, the pronoun determines the person of the verb.

67 The **first person** denotes the person speaking:
I, *Fred Smith,* am willing to go.

68 The **second person** denotes the person or thing spoken **to:**
You, *Henry,* are selected for the honor.

69 The **third person** denotes the person or thing spoken **of:**
Our *coach* is here now; *he* will help us.

70 **Number** shows whether the noun refers to one or to more than one person, place, or thing. There are two classes: **singular, plural.**

71 **Singular number** denotes **one:** *tree, desk, book.*

72 **Plural number** denotes **more than one:** *trees, desks, books.*

Plurals of Nouns

A dictionary is the only complete guide in forming plurals.

73 Form the **plurals of most nouns** by adding *s* to the singular: *bird— birds, tree—trees.*

74 Form the plurals of **nouns ending in ch, sh, s, x and z** by adding *es* to the singular: *church—churches, bush—bushes, guess—guesses, box—boxes, buzz—buzzes.*

75 Form the plurals of **most nouns ending in o preceded by a consonant** by adding *es* to the singular: *hero—heroes, potato—potatoes.*

There are exceptions to this rule, such as: *piano—pianos, solo—solos.*

76 Form the plurals of **nouns ending in o preceded by a vowel** (vowels are *a, e, i, o, u,* and sometimes *w* and *y*) by adding *s* to the singular: *radio—radios, trio—trios.*

The plurals of **a few nouns ending in o** are formed by adding either *s* or *es* to the singular, but *es* is usually preferred: *volcano—volcanoes— volcanos*

77 Form the plurals of **common nouns ending in y preceded by a consonant** by changing *y* to *i* and adding *es: cry—cries, sky—skies.*

Form the plurals of all **proper nouns ending in y** by adding *s:*
We went to the party with the *Kellys.* The three *Henrys* and the two *Marys* were there.

78 Form the plurals of **nouns ending in y preceded by a vowel** by adding only *s: turkey—turkeys, jockey—Jockeys.*

79 Form the plurals of **some nouns ending in f or fe** by changing the *f* or *fe* to *v* and adding *es: sheaf—sheaves, wife—wives, half—halves.*

Other examples are *calf, elf, leaf, life, self, knife, loaf, thief.*

80 Form the plurals of **other nouns ending in f or fe** by adding only *s: fife—fifes, roof—roofs.*

Other examples are *belief, chief, gulf, grief, safe, strife, cliff, proof.*

81 Form the plural of some nouns by changing vowels within them: *goose—geese, mouse—mice, man—men, woman—women.*

82 Form the plurals of a few nouns by adding *en* or *ren: ox—oxen, child—children.*

83 The plurals of **compound nouns** (57) are usually formed by adding *s* or *es* to the main word of the compound; but the plurals of some are formed by adding *s* at the end, and for others the first part of the word is pluralized. In a few cases both words are pluralized: *father-in-law—fathers-in-law, suitcase—suitcases, manservant—menservants.*

84 Form the plurals of **nouns ending in ful** by adding *s* at the end. Do not make the mistake of placing the *s* before the last syllable:

She used three *spoonfuls* (not *spoonsful*) of sugar.

85 Form the plurals of **letters, symbols, figures, and words regarded as words** by adding *'s*, or sometimes just *s:*

Dot your *i's*, cross your *t's*, and make your *3's* (or *3s*) plainer.

You have too many *and's* (or *ands*) in this sentence.

86 Some nouns have the same form in both numbers: *deer, sheep, trout.*

87 Some nouns are plural in form but singular in use: *measles, mumps, ethics.*

88 A few nouns are used in the plural only: *scissors, tongs, trousers.*

89 **Collective nouns** are singular when the group is considered a unit, but plural when the individuals are indicated:

The *team* built *its* reputation on honesty.

The *class* have received *their* diplomas.

90 The **case** of a noun or pronoun shows its relation to other words in the sentence. There are three cases: **nominative, possessive,** and **objective,** but nouns show case only in the possessive form

The nominative and objective "cases" of nouns are merely noun uses, but these terms help explain terms such as *nominative absolute* and *adverbial objective.*

Nominative Case Uses

91 The **subject** of a finite verb is in the nominative case:

Mary sang a song. (A *finite* verb can be used as a predicate; the *infinite* forms—infinitive, participle, and gerund—cannot be used as a predicate.)

92 The **predicate nominative** is in the nominative case:

George is my *friend.*

It was *she.*

He was made *captain.* (280)

A noun or pronoun that completes the meaning of the predicate and denotes the same person or thing as the subject is a **predicate nominative** (sometimes called **subjective complement,** 174-3).

Note: See *predicate adjective* (174-4, 269B, 280).

Diagram—Sentence with a *noun predicate nominative,* or subjective complement:

The girls *were students.*

girls | were \ students
The

Diagram—Sentence with *compound predicate nominative,* or subjective complement:

The trees are *cedars* and *maples.*

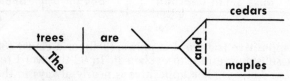

93 **A noun of direct address** is in the nominative case:

Henry, lend me your book.

Will you help me, *Ruth,* with this problem?

Note: The noun of address is used to call the attention of the one spoken to. It is separated from the rest of the sentence by a comma or commas (479).

94 A noun used as an **exclamation** is in the nominative case: *Fire! Fire!*

95 The **nominative absolute** is a noun used in an absolute construction:

The *rain* having ceased, we went home. (478)

The *night* being cold, I wore an overcoat.

Note: The absolute construction is a word or a phrase related to the thought of the sentence in which it is found, but not grammatically related to any word of the sentence. It is usually made up of a noun and a participle (196, 260), either with or without modifiers (7). The absolute construction is easily changed into a clause:

The *work* being completed, we went home.

The *work* completed, we went home. (*Being* is often omitted.)

When the work was completed, we went home. (**clause,** 9, 385)

The absolute construction is set off from the rest of the sentence by a comma (478). Never use a period for this purpose:

Incorrect: The work being completed. We went home.

Correct: The work being completed, we went home.

96 A substantive may be in the nominative case by **apposition:**

Miss Jones, my *teacher,* is in Chicago. (apposition with the subject)

That woman is Miss Jones, my *teacher.* (apposition with predicate nominative)

Note: The substantive used in apposition—an **appositive**—differs from one used in the predicate nominative (92) in that it has no verb to connect it with the word which it explains. In the two illustrations given, *my teacher* is set off by commas and no verb is used to connect *teacher* with *Miss Jones.*

Diagram—Sentence with *noun in apposition with the subject:*
Miss Smith, the *teacher,* bought a book.

Miss Smith (teacher)	bought	book

97   An **appositive** is a word, a phrase (382), or a clause (393-396) placed
after a substantive (45) to explain it. In 96 the word *teacher* explains
who *Miss Jones* is. The appositive is nearly always in the same case as
the word which it explains (but see 113), and it is usually set off by
commas (479):

Miss Jones, my *teacher,* writes books. (**appositive word**)

The fact *that he is coming* makes us happy. (**appositive clause**)

Although the appositive is thought of usually as a substantive (45),
a modifier may be used appositively. The adjective is frequently used
appositively (269A), just as it is often used in the predicate (269B):

The tree, *tall* and *beautiful,* stood near the lake. (*Tall* and *beautiful* are
used appositively to explain the kind of tree.)

The tree near the lake was *tall* and *beautiful.* (*Tall* and *beautiful* are
used in the predicate, 280, to describe *tree,* and the linking verb *was,*
175, is used as a connective.)

Objective Case Uses

98   The **direct object** of a verb is in the objective case:

Mary painted the *picture.*

The direct object is sometimes called the **object complement** (174-1).
it completes the predicate by naming the receiver of the action in the
active voice (179).

99   The direct object of a verb is also said to be in the **accusative case,**
but this term is now seldom used.

100   The **predicate objective,** or **objective complement** (174-2) may
follow verbs of *making, naming, calling, choosing, appointing,* and
so on, after the **direct object;** the second object completes the meaning of the predicate and relates to the direct object.

We elected John *captain.*

101   The **indirect object** is in the objective case:

Mary gave *Alice* a book.

The indirect object may be changed to a prepositional phrase, which
may follow the direct object:

Mary gave a rose to *Alice.*

The preposition (42) used in forming such a phrase is either *to* or *for*.

Diagram—Sentence with *indirect object:*

Mother gave the *boys* some cookies.

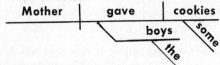

102 The **object of a preposition** is in the objective case:
The bird flew over the *house.* (object of *over*)

103 The **adverbial objective** is a noun used as an adverb:
The child walked three *miles.*   The water was *ankle* deep.

The **adverbial noun** is joined without a preposition to a verb, an adverb, or an adjective to express time, distance, measure, weight, or value. It may be modified by an adjective, such as *three* in the first example.

104 The **subject of an infinitive** (194) is in the objective case:
James believed the *teacher* to be his friend.
There is no need for the *boys* to help.

105 The **complement** of the infinitive *to be* having a subject is in the objective case:

James believed the teacher to be his *friend.*
John thought her to be *me.* (264)

If the infinitive *to be* has no subject, the complement is in the nominative case:

Ann wishes to be the *heroine* in the play.
He was thought to be *I.* (265)

105A The **direct object of an infinitive** is in the objective case:
Helen likes to paint *pictures.*   The judge tried to help *him.*

106 A substantive may be in the objective case by **apposition** (96, 97):
We admire Dr. Brown, our *physician.*
We heard from Mr. Hill, our *principal.*

107 The **object of a participle** (196, 260) is in the objective case:
Waving his *hand,* the boy rode away.

108 The **object of a gerund** (195, 257) is in the objective case:
Playing *games* is interesting.

109 The **cognate object** is in the objective case:
He ran a good *race.*

When the object of a verb expresses an idea similar to that of the verb itself, the object is called **cognate:**

He sleeps a peaceful *sleep.*   He fought a good *fight.*

110 The **retained object** is in the objective case:

I was given a *watch* by my father.

A retained object is one that has been retained after a verb has been changed from active (179) to passive (180) voice:

My father gave (active) me a *watch.* (direct object)
I was given (passive) a *watch* by my father. (retained object)
A watch was given *me* by my father. (retained object)

Note that either the direct or indirect object may be retained.

Possessive Case

111 The **possessive case** denotes ownership, possession, or similar relationship:

This is *Robert's* book.

Note: The possessive case is called the **genitive** by some grammarians.

112 The noun (or pronoun, 141) in the possessive case is used as a modifier, and as a modifier it is sometimes called a **possessive adjective** (122, 126, 141, 261, 272):

He found *Nell's* book. (*Nell's* modifies *book.*)
The *girl's* hair is brown. (*Girl's* modifies *hair.*)

113 A noun in the possessive case may be used as an appositive of another noun (96, 97):

Bob drives his brother *Harry's* car.

Notice that *brother* would have the possessive form if the appositive were omitted.

114 Ownership or possession may be denoted by the noun in a phrase introduced by *of:*

The *poems of Keats,* the *music of Schubert.*

This is the form more commonly used with inanimate things:

The *leaves of the tree* (instead of *the tree's leaves*) are falling.

But many neuter nouns (63) are correctly used in the regular possessive form, although there is no ownership involved. Here are a few of these: *a week's work, a dime's worth, for pity's sake, heart's desire, yesterday's report, time's flight.*

Possessive Forms of Nouns

115   To form the possessive singular of a noun, use an apostrophe and *s* after the word (498): the *boy's* cap, the *girl's* book.

It is permissible to use the apostrophe alone in forming the possessive singular of a noun ending in *s* if the addition of *s* makes pronunciation difficult:

He did this for *Jesus'* sake.

Form the possessive of a noun of two or more syllables ending in *s* or an *s*-sound and not accented on the last syllable usually by adding the apostrophe only:

He did it for his *conscience'* sake.

116   Form the possessive of a plural noun that ends in *s* by adding the apostrophe only:

The two *boys'* caps are torn.
The three *students'* books are here.

117   To form the possessive of a plural noun not ending in *s*, add an apostrophe and *s:*

Men's shoes, *oxen's* horns.

118   In forming the possessive of a compound, place the possessive ending after the last word: *King of England's throne, brother-in-law's farm.*

The possessives of plurals of compounds (83) are formed in the same way:

Brothers-in-law's farms.

119   When two nouns are used to indicate common ownership, the sign of possession is placed after the second noun:

Smith and Brown's office. (Smith and Brown occupy the same office.)

120   When two nouns are used to show separate ownership, add the sign of possession to both nouns:

Opal's and *Edna's* hands are brown.

121   In such phrases as *nobody else,* the possessive is formed by placing the sign at the end of the phrase:

Nobody else's business.

122   A noun or pronoun introducing a gerund (195) is usually in the possessive case:

She told us of *Jane's* winning the prize.
He asked me about *my* writing the story.

PRONOUNS

123 A **pronoun** is a word used to take the place of a noun. Classes of pronouns include the following: **personal, relative, interrogative, demonstrative** (133, 272), **indefinite** (134, 272), **possessive** (126). The last three are sometimes called **pronominal adjectives** (126, 135, 272) because they are used as adjectives when the substantive (45) is expressed.

124 The **antecedent** of a pronoun is the word for which the pronoun stands:

Mary brought her book. (*Mary* is the antecedent of *her*.)

The *girl* who came here has gone. (The antecedent of *who* is *girl*.)

125 A pronoun generally agrees with its antecedent in **gender, person,** and **number.** Its case is determined by its use in a particular group of words. Modifications of the pronoun are the same as those of the noun: **gender, person, number,** and **case.**

126 The **absolute possessive pronoun** represents the possessor and the thing possessed. It does not modify a noun directly.

This book is *mine*. (The word *mine* here is equivalent to *my* book; therefore it represents both the possessor and the thing possessed.)

The absolute possessive pronouns are *mine, yours, his, hers, its, theirs, ours*.

Some authorities class as **possessive adjectives** (141) the forms *my, your, his, her, its, our, their*, when used as modifiers. However, these remain pronouns, agreeing with their antecedents in gender, person, and number, even while modifying nouns.

127 **Personal pronouns** show by their form whether they are the first, second, or third person (66-69). The simple personal pronouns include *I, you, he, she, it, we, they,* and their inflected forms (139).

128 **Compound personal pronouns** are formed by adding *-self* or *-selves* to some of the simple personals: *myself, yourself, himself, herself, itself, ourselves, themselves*.

Never use *hisself* or *theirselves*.

129 A compound personal pronoun is used correctly as a **reflexive** to refer an action back to the subject of a sentence:

He helped *himself*.

It is also correctly used as an **intensive** for emphasis:

He *himself* is wrong.

It is preferable not to use a compound personal pronoun to take the place of a simple personal pronoun:

John and *I* (not *myself*) went to the show.

130   A **relative pronoun** is not only a pronoun but also a connecting word. It refers to a substantive (45) in the main clause (386) in which it is found, and it joins an adjective clause (397) to its antecedent. The relative pronoun has a use in the dependent clause (387, 155), such as subject, object of verb, or object of preposition, and it joins the dependent clause to an independent, or main, clause. Because the relative pronoun connects a subordinate clause with a main clause, it is called also a **conjunctive pronoun.** Words used as relative pronouns are *who, whom, whose, which, that,* and *what* (*what* has no antecedent):

The boy *who* sang is here.

131   The **compound relative pronoun** is formed by adding -*ever* or -*soever* to certain simple relatives. The case of a relative pronoun depends on its use in its own clause:

We invite *whoever* will come. (*Whoever* is the subject of *will* come.)

132   The **interrogative pronouns** are *who, whom, whose, which,* and *what,* when used in asking questions:

Who is the speaker?

133   **Demonstrative** or **adjective pronouns** (123, 134, 135, 281) point out particular persons, places, or things:

This is my pencil. *That* is your book.

Note: The most commonly used demonstratives are *this, that, these,* and *those.* When one of these words modifies a substantive (45), it ceases to be a pronoun and becomes an adjective (135, 266, 272, 281):

That is a beautiful tree. (**pronoun**)   *That* tree is beautiful. (**adjective**)

134   **Indefinite pronouns** point out persons, places, or things less clearly than demonstratives do (133):

Each should do his work.   *Many* were absent today.

Note: Some of the commonly used indefinites are *everybody, everyone, anybody, nobody, each, either, neither, one, none, some, other, another, few, all, many, several,* and *both.* When one of these words modifies a substantive (45), it ceases to be a pronoun (123) and becomes an adjective (135, 266, 272, 281):

Many attended the lecture today. (**pronoun**)
Many students attended the lecture today. (**adjective**)
Some do not like this story. (**pronoun**)
Some students do not like this story. (**adjective**)

135   Words which are sometimes used as adjectives and sometimes as pronouns are sometimes called **pronominal adjectives** or **adjective pronouns** (123, 133, 134, 272):

Each man did his duty.   *Each* did his duty.

136 In using relative pronouns (130), *who* is generally used to refer to persons; *which,* to animals and things; and *that,* to either persons, animals, places, or things:

This is the man *who* helped us.
The dog, *which* is a faithful animal, is loved by man.
He spoke of the men and the ships *that* were lost.

137 Make the pronoun agree with its antecedent (124) in number (70):

Each boy should study *his* (not *their*) lesson. (*Boy* is singular and calls for a singular pronoun.)

Case

138 The case forms of pronouns are always determined by their own use in a sentence, never by the use of their antecedent.

Was it he *whom* they saw? (*Whom* is the object of *saw.*)

139 The nominative case forms of the personal pronouns are *I, we, he, she, they;* the objective case forms are *me, us, him, her, them.* The forms *it* and *you* are used in both nominative and objective case. *Her* is either objective or possessive.

Declension of Personal Pronouns

	Singular			Plural		
	Nominative	Possessive	Objective	Nominative	Possessive	Objective
1st per.	I	my, mine	me	we	our, ours	us
2nd per.	you	your, yours	you	you	your, yours	you
3rd per.	he	his	him	they	their, theirs	them
	she	her, hers	her	they	their, theirs	them
	it	its	it	they	their, theirs	them

140 Personal pronouns (127) in the **nominative case** have the same uses as nouns (91-97), as follows:

1. **Subject of a verb:** *I* went home.
2. **Predicate nominative:** I am *he.*
3. **Direct address:** *You,* Fred, can give a demonstration.
4. **Exclamation:** Lucky *he!*
5. **Nominative absolute:** *He* being ill, we did not go.
6. **Appositive:** We, John and *I,* played ball.
7. **Complement of the infinitive *to be* not having a subject:** John was thought to be *I.* (See 105, 265.)

141 Personal pronouns (127) in the **possessive case do not require the sign of possession** as do nouns. The possessive forms (see 126, 139) are *my, mine, our, ours, his, her, hers, their, theirs, its, your, yours:*

The bird sang *its* (not *it's*) song.

The only correct use of the apostrophe with the personal pronouns is in contractions:

It's time to go home.

These pronouns in the possessive case are sometimes called **possessive adjectives:** *my, your, his, her, our, their, its.* (126, 272)

142 Personal pronouns in the **objective case** (139) may be used in these ways:

1. **Direct object of a verb:** The teacher praised *him.*
2. **Indirect object:** He gave *her* a diamond.
3. **Object of a preposition:** I spoke to *him.*
4. **Subject of an infinitive:** He asked *me* to stay.
5. **Complement of the infinitive *to be* having a subject:** Did you think Sally to be *her?* (105, 264.)
6. **Object of a participle:** Seeing *me* at the door, my aunt smiled happily.
7. **Object of an infinitive:** Mary tried to help *me.* (105A)
8. **Object of a gerund:** Helping *him* was my duty. (108, 195, 257)
9. **Appositive:** Ann invited us, Bill and *me.*

143 A noun or pronoun following *than* or *as* is in the nominative or objective case according to its construction in the elliptical (5) clause for which it stands:

You are stronger that *he* (is strong).

You like her better than (you like) *me.*

144 When a subject or a predicate nominative is compound (17, 92), both parts should be in the nominative case form:

John and *he* are going.

The winners are Bill and *she.*

145 Do not repeat a subject by using a pronoun after it:

Charles (not *Charles he*) studied hard.

146 When a pronoun is used as subject or as predicate nominative and has a noun in apposition (96, 97) following it, the nominative form (139) of the pronoun should be used:

All *we* girls went to the show.

It was *we* boys who did the work.

147 A personal pronoun used as a **predicate nominative** should be in nominative case form (139, 175):

The guests were *she* (not *her*) and *they* (not *them*).

Note: Some good authorities feel that "It is *me*" is more natural in colloquial language than "It is *I*," but most textbook writers insist on "It is *I*" in formal written work.

148 If a pronoun appears in a **compound object of a verb** or a **compound object of a preposition,** the pronoun should be in the objective case form:

Our uncle saw Clyde and *me.*   The woman spoke to Grace and *me.*

149 When the **indirect object** (101) is compound, all pronoun parts should be in the objective case form:

The farmer gave *her* and *me* some apples.

150 When a pronoun is the direct (142-1) or the indirect (142-2) object of a verb and has a noun in apposition (97), use the objective form of the pronoun:

Our teacher saw *us* girls.   Bob sent *us* boys a message.

151 *But,* when used in the sense of *except,* is a preposition (332) and must, like *except* and *between,* have an object:

He stood between you and *me.*   I invited all the girls but *her.*

152 If a pronoun is the object of a preposition (142-3) and has a noun in apposition (97), use the objective form of the pronoun:

Sue came with *us* students.

153 *Who, whom, whose, which,* and *what* when used in asking questions are **interrogative pronouns.**

154 *Who,* whether interrogative or relative, is the nominative case form:

Who did Wilma say was the speaker? (*Who* is the subject of *was;* the clause is the object of *say.*)

Whom is the objective case form:
Whom will you send to town?
I met the girl of *whom* you spoke. (**relative**)

Declension of Relative Pronouns

Singular and Plural

Nominative	Possessive	Objective
who	whose	whom
which	whose	which

155   The case form of the pronoun used as a **relative** (130) depends upon the use of the relative in the clause (9) it introduces:

This is the boy *who* lost his book. (*who* is subject of *lost*.)

The man *whom* you saw is my friend. (*whom* is object of saw.)

156   The compound relative *whoever* is the nominative case form:

Stop *whoever* comes this way. (*Whoever* is the subject of *comes*. The clause *whoever comes this way* is the object of *stop*.)

157   The compound relative *whomever* is the objective case form:

Send it to *whomever* you choose. (*Whomever* is the object of *choose*. The clause *whomever you choose* is the object of the preposition *to*.)

Whomever you ask will be received. (*Whomever* is the object of *ask*. The clause *whomever you ask* is the subject of the verb *will be received*.)

Note: The case forms of the compound relative *whoever* seem more easily confused than the forms of *who*. When the compound relatives are used, the form may be determined more readily if words are supplied to show an antecedent. In 156, for example, the sentence would be expanded to *You stop him who comes this way*. The example in this section would be *He whom you ask will be received*.

Number

158   The indefinite pronouns *each, either, neither, everyone, anyone, someone, nobody, no one,* and *everybody* are singular:

Each should do *his* best.   Neither could sing *his* song.

159   A pronoun must be singular when it refers to a noun modified by such indefinite adjectives (134, 135) as *each, every,* and *neither:*

Each boy brought *his* ticket.   Every girl brought *her* books.

Sometimes the meaning is so clearly plural that a singular personal pronoun cannot be used to refer to the indefinite pronoun:

Everyone was so busy writing the story that *they* did not notice who had come in. (Not *he* did not notice)

However, this may be rewritten:

Everyone was so busy writing the story that *nobody* noticed who had come in.

160   A pronoun which refers to a collective noun (56) is singular if the group acts as a unit:

The band has won fame because of *its* leader.

But the pronoun is plural if the individuals of the group act as individuals:

The band have ordered *their* new instruments.

Usage

161   Some authorities feel that *which* should not be used to refer to a complete statement (366):

Questioned: He had to work, *which* caused him to be late.

Better: He was late *because* he had to work.

162   The word *same* should not be used as a pronoun instead of *it* or *them:*

I have read your offer and have decided to accept *it* (not *the same*).

163   *Them* should not be used as an adjective nor as the subject of a sentence:

Those (not *Them* or *Them there*) books are mine.

164   *They* should not be used with indefinite reference:

People (not *They*) say that he is talented.

VERBS

165   A **verb** (39) is a word that expresses action, being, or state of being. (A verb may be formed by a group of words. Such a group is called a **verb phrase** or a **phrasal verb**—176, 380.) According to the way in which they form their principal parts (197), verbs are divided into two classes: **regular** (weak) and **irregular** (strong).

166   A **regular verb** forms its past tense (188) and past participle (196) by adding *d, ed,* or *t* to the present tense (186): *hear—heard—heard, help—helped—helped, deal—dealt—dealt.*

167   An **irregular** (strong) **verb** usually forms its past tense and past participle by changing a vowel of the present (or infinitive, 194) form: *begin—began—begun.*

Sometimes a different word may be used for a principal part: *go—went—gone.*

Sometimes all the principal parts are the same: *set—set—set.*

Transitive and Intransitive

168   According to use, verbs are classified as **transitive** or **intransitive**.

169   The **transitive verb** has a receiver of the action to complete its meaning. When the actor is the subject (3), the receiver of the action is the object (6):

Bob *sang* a song.

When the receiver of the action is the subject, the verb is in the **passive voice** (180) and remains transitive:

A song was *sung* by Bob.

The verb *was sung* is in the passive voice. When the subject is the receiver of the action, the name of the actor may not be expressed:
Many songs *were sung*.

170 An **intransitive verb** does not have a receiver of the action:
The eagle *flew* over the mountain.

171 A verb may be used as transitive in one sentence and as intransitive in another sentence:
She *sings* well. (**intransitive**)
She *sings* beautiful songs. (**transitive**)

172 Intransitive verbs are of two classes: **complete** and **linking.**

173 A **complete verb** is an intransitive verb which makes a complete statement without the help of any other word:
Birds *fly*. Fish *swim*.
The horse *drinks*. Children *play*.

174 A verb sometimes takes a substantive (45) or an adjective (40, 266) to complete its meaning. The substantive or adjective added is called a **complement.** There are several classes of complements:

1. **Direct object** (98) or object complement:
Bob caught the *ball*.
Many won the *trophy*.

2. **Predicate objective** (100) or objective complement:
They elected him *captain*.
We appointed him *leader*.

3. **Predicate nominative** (92) or subjective complement:
Poe was a great *poet*.
The man became a *leader*.

4. **Predicate adjective** (280). The predicate adjective completes the predicate of the sentence and modifies, describes, or points out the subject of the sentence:
The roses are *beautiful*. (The predicate adjective *beautiful* completes the verb *are* and describes the subject *roses*.)
The apple looks *good*. (280)

Diagram—Sentence with *predicate adjective:*
The old woman was very *sad*.

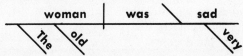

175 A **linking verb** is an intransitive verb which connects the subject with a predicate substantive (45) or a predicate adjective (280). The substantive or adjective following the linking verb either means the same as the subject or describes, limits, or points out the subject:

Webster *was* a statesman.

The rose *is* beautiful.

The most commonly used linking verb is *be* in its various forms such as *am, is, was, were.* Some other verbs used as linking verbs are *seem, become, appear, prove, look, remain, feel, taste, smell, sound, turn, grow.*

A noun or pronoun joined to a subject by a linking verb is in the nominative case (92, 140-2, 147):

It is *he.*

That was *she.*

Auxiliaries

176   An **auxiliary verb** is a verb which helps another verb. A verb with its helper or helpers is a **verb phrase** (39, 380-5). Some verbs used as auxiliaries are *do, did, be* (and its various forms), *have, may, can, must, will, shall, might, could, would,* and *should.* Some of these verbs serve not only as auxiliaries but also as main verbs:

Jack *did* bring his book. (**auxiliary**)

Jack *did* good work. (**main verb**)

177   Although the linking verb *be* (175) **does not take objects,** all forms of this verb may become auxiliaries in forming transitive verbs (169):

It *is* she. (**linking**)

Ruth *is* writing a letter. (*Is* is an **auxiliary** used in forming the verb phrase *is writing,* which is a transitive verb with an object *letter.*)

The forms of *be* are also used as auxiliaries in forming the passive voice (180).

The house *was* destroyed by fire.

The report *has been* received.

178   The modifications of a verb show **voice, mood, tense, person,** and **number.**

Voice

179   **Voice** depends on whether the subject of the verb acts or is acted upon. **Active voice** denotes that the subject of the verb is the actor:

The man *called* the dog.

180   **Passive voice** denotes that the subject receives the action:

The dog *was called* by the man.

The passive always has a verb phrase (39, 176, 380) composed of a form of the auxiliary (176) *be* followed by a past participle (196):

The letter *has been written* by the manager.

Note: Passive verbs sometimes have two receivers of the action: the subject and the retained object (110):

He was given a *scholarship*.

Mood

181 Mood indicates the manner in which the action is conceived.

182 The **indicative mood** makes a statement or asks a question:
He *is* my friend. *Is* she a teacher?

183 The **imperative mood** gives a command or makes a request:
Shut the door.
Will you kindly *return* the book. (Note that a question mark is not used.)

184 The **subjunctive mood** expresses doubt or a wish or condition contrary to fact:
I wish I *were* a lawyer.
If I *were* you, I should go.

The present subjunctive occurs after verbs like *demand* (250):
I insist that he *go*.

Tense

185 Tense denotes the time of the action indicated by a verb. The time is not always the same as that indicated by the name of the tense.

186 The **present tense** may express action which is going on at the present time or which occurs always, repeatedly, or habitually:
He *sees* the train.
He *eats* cereal for breakfast every day.

The present tense may express future time:
The train *leaves* in five minutes.

It may be used as a historical present, referring to the past:
The detective *solves* the mystery just in time.

187 The **present perfect tense** expresses action completed at the present time or continuing into the present:
He *has written* a letter to his uncle. (**completed**)
I *have lived* here for many years. (**continuing**)

188 The **past tense** expresses action completed at a definite time in the past:

He *wrote* the letter yesterday.

Do not use the past tense for the present perfect:

Joe *has* (not *did*) not come yet.

189 The **past perfect tense** expresses action completed before a certain time in the past:

He *had written* the letter before I saw him.

190 The **future tense** expresses action which will take place in the future:

He *will write* the letter tomorrow.

191 The **future perfect tense** expresses action which will be completed before a certain time in the future:

He *will have written* the letter before we arrive tomorrow.

192 A **verb** as a rule agrees with its subject in person (66-69) and number (70-72). Failure to observe this rule causes many errors:

He *doesn't* (not *don't*) know what to do.

(See 229-242, 253, and other sections under "Verb agreement" in the index.)

Verbals

193 There are three verb forms, called **verbals**, which are used as other parts of speech: **infinitive, gerund,** and **participle.**

194 The **infinitive** (256) is the form of the verb usually introduced by *to* (see 225):

We like *to play* basketball.

The **present infinitive** is the same as the basic present-tense form of the verb, usually preceded by *to: to see, to go, to do.*

The **perfect infinitive** is formed by placing *to have* before the past participle (196): *to have seen, to have gone, to have done.*

195 The **gerund** (54, 257-259) is a verbal noun ending in *ing*. The gerund may, like any verb, take an object. It may be modified by an adjective or an adverb. A gerund is sometimes referred to as a **parti-**

cipial noun, because in reality it is a participle used as a noun. The gerund is the name of an action:

Trying is commendable. (*Trying* is the subject of the sentence.)

Don enjoys *reading* history. (*Reading* is the object of the verb *enjoys* and it has its own object *history*.)

Walking rapidly is good exercise. (The adverb *rapidly* modifies the gerund *walking*.)

196 A **participle** is a verbal (193) which has some of the properties of a verb and some of the properties of an adjective. It is used, like an adjective, to modify a noun or a pronoun; and it may, like a verb, take an object:

The boy *waving* the flag is Robert. (*Waving* modifies *boy* as an adjective and takes an object *flag* as a verb.)

The **present participle** ends in *ing* and generally describes action going on at the same time as other action, but it sometimes refers to time preceding that of the verb used as predicate:

Standing at the window, I saw the parade.

Sitting here, we see the parade.

The present participle is used in progressive verb phrases (205).
The **past participle** generally indicates completed action.
The past participle of a regular verb (166) has in general the same form as the past tense (188), but the forms of the past participle of the irregular verbs (167) show variety (199):

This was a work *done* for others.

The terms *suggested* by the committee were fair.

The past participle form is always used after *has, have,* and *had* to form the perfect tenses (187, 189, 191).

The **perfect participle** is formed of *having* and the past participle:

Having done the work, the boys went home.

Principal Parts

197 The **principal parts** of a verb are the first person (67) singular (71) of the present (186) indicative (182), the first person singular of the past (188) indicative, and the past participle (196):

I *go*—I *went*—I have *gone*.   I *see*—I *saw*—I have *seen*.

198 Do not confuse the principal parts of irregular verbs (167):

I *saw* (not *seen*) him yesterday.

199 Principal Parts of the Most Difficult Verbs

Present Tense	Past Tense	Past Participle	Present Tense	Past Tense	Past Participle
am, be	was, were	been	know	knew	known
begin	began	begun	lay	laid	laid
beat	beat	beaten	lead	led	led
bite	bit	bitten, bit	lend	lent	lent
blow	blew	blown	lie (recline)	lay	lain
break	broke	broken	lie	lied	lied
bring	brought	brought	raise	raised	raised
build	built	built	ride	rode	ridden
burst	burst	burst	ring	rang	rung
catch	caught	caught	rise	rose	risen
choose	chose	chosen	run	ran	run
come	came	come	see	saw	seen
dive	dived	dived	set	set	set
do	did	done	shake	shook	shaken
drag	dragged	dragged	sing	sang, sung	sung
draw	drew	drawn	sink	sank, sunk	sunk
drink	drank	drunk	sit	sat	sat
drown	drowned	drowned	sling	slung	slung
drive	drove	driven	speak	spoke	spoken
eat	ate	eaten	spring	sprang, sprung	sprung
fall	fell	fallen			
fight	fought	fought	sting	stung	stung
flee	fled	fled	steal	stole	stolen
flow	flowed	flowed	swear	swore	sworn
fly	flew	flown	swim	swam	swum
forsake	forsook	forsaken	swing	swung	swung
freeze	froze	frozen	take	took	taken
give	gave	given	tear	tore	torn
go	went	gone	throw	threw	thrown
grow	grew	grown	wake	waked, woke	waked
hang	hung	hung			
hang (execute)	hanged	hanged	wear	wore	worn
			weave	wove	woven
hear	heard	heard	wring	wrung	wrung
hide	hid	hidden, hid	write	wrote	written

Conjugation

200 The **conjugation** of a verb is the orderly arrangement of its forms through its voices (179-180), moods (181-184), tenses (185-191), persons (66-69, 192), and numbers (70-72, 192).

201 CONJUGATION OF THE VERB *TO BE*

INDICATIVE MOOD Singular Plural

Present Tense
	Singular	Plural
	1. I am	1. We are
	2. You are	2. You are
	3. He is	3. They are

Past Tense
	Singular	Plural
	1. I was	1. We were
	2. You were	2. You were
	3. He was	3. They were

Future Tense
	Singular	Plural
	1. I shall be	1. We shall be
	2. You will be	2. You will be
	3. He will be	3. They will be

Present Perfect Tense
	Singular	Plural
	1. I have been	1. We have been
	2. You have been	2. You have been
	3. He has been	3. They have been

Past Perfect Tense
	Singular	Plural
	1. I had been	1. We had been
	2. You had been	2. You had been
	3. He had been	3. They had been

Future Perfect Tense
	Singular	Plural
	1. I shall have been	1. We shall have been
	2. You will have been	2. You will have been
	3. He will have been	3. They will have been

SUBJUNCTIVE MOOD

Present Tense
	Singular	Plural
	1. I be	1. We be
	2. You be	2. You be
	3. He be	3. They be

Past Tense
	Singular	Plural
	1. I were	1. We were
	2. You were	2. You were
	3. He were	3. They were

Present Perfect Tense
	Singular	Plural
	1. I have been	1. We have been
	2. You have been	2. You have been
	3. He have been	3. They have been

Past Perfect Tense
	Singular	Plural
	1. I had been	1. We had been
	2. You had been	2. You had been
	3. He had been	3. They had been

IMPERATIVE MOOD

Present Tense Be Be

	Present	Past	Perfect
INFINITIVES	To be		To have been
PARTICIPLES	Being	Been	Having been
GERUNDS	Being		Having been

CONJUGATION OF THE VERB *TO SEE*
202   Active Voice

INDICATIVE MOOD

		Singular	*Plural*
Present Tense		1. I see	1. We see
		2. You see	2. You see
		3. He sees	3. They see
Past Tense		1. I saw	1. We saw
		2. You saw	2. You saw
		3. He saw	3. They saw
Future Tense		1. I shall see	1. We shall see
		2. You will see	2. You will see
		3. He will see	3. They will see
Present Perfect Tense		1. I have seen	1. We have seen
		2. You have seen	2. You have seen
		3. He has seen	3. They have seen
Past Pefect Tense		1. I had seen	1. We had seen
		2. You had seen	2. You had seen
		3. He had seen	3. They had seen
Future Perfect Tense		1. I shall have seen	1. We shall have seen
		2. You will have seen	2. You will have seen
		3. He will have seen	3. They will have seen

SUBJUNCTIVE MOOD

		Singular	*Plural*
Present Tense		1. I see	1. We see
		2. You see	2. You see
		3. He sees	3. They see
Past Tense		1. I saw	1. We saw
		2. You saw	2. You saw
		3. He saw	3. They saw
Present Perfect Tense		1. I had been	1. We have seen
		2. You have seen	2. You have seen
		3. He have seen	3. They have seen
Past Perfect Tense		1. I had seen	1. We had seen
		2. You had seen	2. You had seen
		3. He had seen	3. They had seen

IMPERATIVE MOOD

	See	See

	Present	*Past*	*Perfect*
INFINITIVES	To see		To have seen
PARTICIPLES	Seeing	Seen	Having seen
GERUNDS	Seeing		Having seen

CONJUGATION OF THE VERB *TO SEE*

203 Passive Voice

INDICATIVE MOOD

	Singular	Plural
	1. I am seen	1. We are seen
Present Tense	2. You are seen	2. You are seen
	3. He is seen	3. They are seen
	1. I was seen	1. We were seen
Past Tense	2. You were seen	2. You were seen
	3. He was seen	3. They were seen
	1. I shall be seen	1. We shall be seen
Future Tense	2. You will be seen	2. You will be seen
	3. He will be seen	3. They will be seen
	1. I have been seen	1. We have been seen
Present Perfect Tense	2. You have been seen	2. You have been seen
	3. He has been seen	3. They had been seen
	1. I had been seen	1. We had been seen
Past Perfect Tense	2. You had been seen	2. You had been seen
	3. He had been seen	3. They had been seen
	1. I shall have been seen	1. We shall have been seen
Future Perfect Tense	2. You will have been seen	3. They will have been seen
	3. He will have been seen	2. You will have been seen

SUBJUNCTIVE MOOD

	Singular	Plural
	1. I be seen	1. We be seen
Present Tense	2. You be seen	2. You be seen
	3. He be seen	3. They be seen
	1. I were seen	1. We were seen
Past Tense	2. You were seen	2. You were seen
	3. He were seen	3. They were seen
	1. I have been seen	1. We have been seen
Present Perfect Tense	2. You have been seen	2. You have been seen
	3. He have been seen	3. They have been seen
	1. I had been seen	1. We had been seen
Past Perfect Tense	2. You had been seen	2. You had been seen
	3. He had been seen	3. They had been seen

IMPERATIVE MOOD

	Singular	Plural
Present Tense	Be seen	Be seen

	Present	**Past**	**Perfect**
INFINITIVES	To be seen		To have been seen
PARTICIPLES	Being seen	Seen	Having been seen
GERUNDS	Being seen		Having been seen

204   Besides the tense forms given above, two other forms are frequently used: the **progressive** and the **emphatic.**

205   The **progressive form** represents action as continuing at the time noted. It is made by placing some form of the verb *to be,* such as *is, was, were,* and *are,* before the present participle (196):

I *am seeing*—you *are seeing*—he *is seeing.*

Although the present-participle form is used in making the progressive verb phrase, the participle is considered not as a participle but as a part of the entire verb phrase:

Esther *is painting* a picture. (*Painting,* the present-participle form, is here considered a part of the verb phrase *is painting.*)

206   The **emphatic form** gives emphasis to the present or past form of the verb in the active voice (179) by the use of *do, does,* or *did:* Forms of *do* are used also in negative statements and in questions without emphasis:

I *do see.* He *did see.* (**emphatic**)
Do you see? I *do* not see. (**not emphatic**)

207   The **synopsis** of a verb is the correct arrangement of its moods (182-184), voices (179-180), and tenses (186-191) **in one person** (66) **and number** (70); it is an abbreviated conjugation (200).

208   SYNOPSIS OF THE VERB *TO SEE*
in the 3rd Person singular Number

INDICATIVE MOOD

	Active	Passive
Present Tense	He sees	He is seen
Past Tense	He saw	He was seen
Future Tense	He will see	He will be seen
Present Perfect Tense	He has seen	He has been seen
Past Perfect Tense	He had seen	He had been seen
Future Perfect Tense	He will have seen	He will have been seen

SUBJUNCTIVE MOOD

Present Tense	He see	He be seen
Past Tense	He saw	He were seen
Present Perfect Tense	He have seen	He have been seen
Past Perfect Tense	He had seen	He had been seen

(The imperative mood is used in the second person only.)

Usage

209 Five frequently used verbs that cause much trouble are the following: *come, go do, see, give.*

> Bob *came* (not *come*) yesterday.
> He had *come* (not *came*) when I left.
> She had *gone* (not *went*) when you came.
> May *did* (not *done*) the work well.
> She has *done* (not *did*) good work.
> I *saw* (not *seen*) her yesterday.
> Tom had *seen* (not *saw*) the show.
> Ann *gave* (not *give*) me this rose.
> Nell had *given* (not *gave*) her a flower.

210 These three pairs of verbs cause much confusion: *lie—lay, sit—set, rise—raise.*

Lie, sit, and *rise* are always intransitive (170) in their usual meanings. *Lay, set,* and *raise* are usually transitive (169) and, therefore, must have an object to complete the meaning:

> Let us *lie* here and rest. I *laid* the book here yesterday.
> She *sits* by the window to read. I *set* the box on the shelf.
> The cake did not *rise* well. Did you *raise* the flag?

Note: the verbs *lay* and *set* may be used as intransitives in certain meanings:

> The hen *lays* well.
> The sun *set* at six o'clock yesterday.
> This jelly did not *set* well.
> We eagerly *set* out on our long journey.

211 *May* is used to express permission; *can* refers to ability:

> *May* I go to town? *Can* the bird fly?

Some writers use *can* for permission, but this usage is often disapproved.

212 Use *shall* in the first person and *will* in the second and third persons for the simple future tense:

> I *shall* sing this afternoon.
> You *will* succeed.
> He *will* stay at home.

213 To express determination, desire, or a promise, reverse the normal order and use *will* in the first person and *shall* in the second and third persons:

> I *will* be there.
> You *shall* pay me what you owe me.
> They *shall* be brought to justice.

214 In asking questions in the first person, use *shall;* in the second or third person, use the form which would be correct in the answer:

Shall you leave tomorrow? (The answer is "I *shall*.")
Will John defy me? (He *will*.)

215 Use *shall* in all persons in object (noun) clauses after verbs of deciding, wishing, demanding, willing, etc.:

He insists that they *shall* not follow him.

216 In an indirect quotation (the thought but not the words of the speaker) use the tense form correct for the speaker:

John says that he *shall* win. (He said, "I *shall* win.")

217 The uses of *should* and *would* correspond to those of *shall* and *will:*

1. For simple future, use *should* with the first person, and use *would* with the second and third.

2. For determination, reverse the order.

3. In questions in the first person, use *should*. (See 214.) In questions in the second and third persons, use the form which would be correct in the answer.

4. In indirect discourse, use the form which would be correct if the quotation were direct.

Note: There is a tendency even among conservative authorities not to stress the foregoing rules governing the use of *shall* and *will*, *should* and *would*, because of the variation in actual practice.

218 *Had ought to* is never correct as a combination for *ought to* or *should:*

He *should* (or *ought to*, not *had ought to*) work.

219 The use of the word *loan* as a verb is interchangeable with *lend* in matters of money but is more restricted in other meanings:

He *loaned* me ten dollars.

220 Do not confuse *leave* and *let*, *learn* and *teach*. *To leave* means *to go away from; to let* means *to permit* or *to allow:*

She will *let* (not *leave*) us use her pen.

To learn means *to get information; to teach* means *to give information:*

He will *teach* (not *learn*) me to paint.

221 *Accept* and *except* are often confused. *To accept* means *to take; to except* means *to leave out:*

I *accept* the gift.
If we *except* her, she will feel hurt.

222 Although *ain't* is usually condemned, we need some good word to take its place (560):

The roses *aren't* (not *ain't*) in bloom yet.

I am to blame, *am I not* (not *ain't I*)?

Note: In England the form *aren't I* is considered correct in the preceding sentence. Although this form seems to be gaining in favor in this country, many leading American authorities still class it with *ain't*.

223 Do not use *of* as a substitute for *have:*

She should not *have* (not *of*) gone home.

224 Some authorities object to the use of *and* for *to* with *try:*

Questioned: Try *and* help her.

Correct: Try *to* help her.

And is never used with *tries, tried,* or *trying.*

225 After certain words the *to* is generally omitted from the infinitive (194). Some of these words are *bid, dare, let, make, help, need, see:*

Let us (to) go to the show.

226 There is some objection to the use of *but what* after negative forms of verbs:

Questioned: He did not know *but what* I won.

Informal: He did not know *but that* I won.

Formal: He did not know *that* I won.

227 Do not use *help but* in the sense of *avoid* in formal writing:

Colloquial: He could not *help but* laugh.

Formal: He could not *help* laughing.

228 The **split infinitive**—the use of a word between the parts of an infinitive (194)—is not incorrect, but may be awkward:

Awkward: She told me *to not help* him.

Better: She told me *not to help* him.

Agreement of Verb and Subject

229 Words joined to a subject by *with, accompanied by, together with, as well as, no less than,* or *including* do not change the number of the subject:

The teacher, as well as the students, *was* there.

230 Two or more singular subjects joined by *or* or *nor* require a singular verb:

Neither Esther nor Ruth *was* present.

231 If a subject is composed of both singular and plural forms joined by *or* or *nor*, the verb must agree with the nearer:

Neither he nor the boys *play* golf. The other boys or Henry *is* to blame.

232 In a sentence beginning with *here* or *there*, the number of the verb is determined by the number of the substantive following it:

There *is* a book on the table. There *are* hats in the window.
Here *are* Bob and Sue. There *go* Joe and Fred.

Note: When *there* is used as an introductory word, as in the first two sentences, it is called an **expletive.** An expletive is a word which, without special meaning of its own, points ahead to a subject or object. *It* is another word frequently used as an expletive:

It is good to be here. Make *it* clear that she is invited.

233 A collective noun (56) takes a singular verb when the group is considered a unit and takes a plural verb when the individuals are considered (89):

Our football team *is* popular. The team *have* received their sweaters.

234 In expressions like *one of the girls who, one of the trees which,* and *one of the persons that,* the verb in the relative clause agrees with the antecedent of the relative pronoun (130):

She is one of those teachers who *are* inspiring. (The antecedent of *who* is *teachers.*)
She is the only one of them who *understands.* (The antecedent of *who* is *one.*)

235 *Each, either, neither, someone, somebody, anyone, anybody, everyone, everybody, no one, nobody, one,* and *a person* are singular (158, 159):

Each of the students *was* (not *were*) questioned.
Everyone opened *his* book and *was* ready.

236 If *plenty, abundance,* or *rest* is modified by a phrase introduced by *of,* the verb agrees with the noun in the phrase:

Plenty of potatoes *are* grown in Colorado.
Plenty of meat *was* provided.

Note: Fractions are used in this same way:

One third of the paper *was* sold. One fifth of the boats *were* lost.

237 If the noun *number* is preceded by *a* and followed by *of,* it usually takes a plural verb; if it is preceded by *the,* it requires a singular verb:

A number of men *were* hurt. The number of accidents *is* great.

238 A noun which means an amount of money, a space of time, or a unit of measurement is singular in meaning even when the form is plural:

Fifty cents *is* the price.   Ten miles *is* a long way to walk.

239 A phrase (380) between the subject (except as given in 236) and the verb does not affect the verb:

One of the girls *is* my friend.

240 If the subject of the verb is made up of two or more words joined by *and,* the verb is plural. (If the two are thought of as a unit, the verb is singular: Bread and butter *is* a good food.) In asking questions beginning with verbs, it is necessary to be careful:

Helen and Grace *are* here.   *Are* Grace and her sister here?

241 If a subject consists of two or more nouns, only one of which is expressed, the verb is plural:

A red and a blue book *are* on the desk.

242 A verb used with a relative pronoun (130) has the same number and person as the noun or pronoun to which the relative refers:

He gave the book to me who *am* its owner.

Sequence of Tenses

243 If the verb in the main clause (386) is in the past tense (188), the verb in the dependent clause (387) may be in the past tense:

Paul said that he *expected* to win.

244 The past tense in the main clause (386) may be followed by the present tense in the dependent clause (387) when it expresses a general truth:

Columbus believed that the earth *is* round.

Note: An idea once established as truth, now known to be untrue, is expressed in the past tense:

The ancients believed that the earth *was* flat.

Special Uses of Voice, Tense, Number

245 Do not shift illogically from the active voice (179) to the passive (180):

As we came over the hill, we *saw a deer* (not a *deer was seen*).

246 Use the active voice (179) unless there is some good reason for using the passive:

We *heard a noise* (not A *noise was heard*).

247 In expressing a **wish or a condition** contrary to fact, use *were,* not *was:*

If I *were* he, I'd go home.   I wish he *were* the governor.

248 In a past **condition not contrary to fact,** the indicative mood (182) is used, not the subjunctive (184) as in 247:

If John *was* present, I did not see him.

249 After *as if* and *as though,* use the subjunctive *were:*

She speaks as though she *were* angry.

250 With words expressing **command or necessity,** use either the present subjunctive form (184) or a verb phrase:

It is necessary that the boy be (or *should be*) punished for the crime.
It was necessary that he *be* punished.

251 Use *are* or *were* with *you,* even when the pronoun is singular:

Edgar, you *were* there.

252 When one subject is affirmative and the other negative, **the verb agrees with the affirmative:**

His honesty, not her tears, *causes* me to relent.

253 In the use of the **arithmetical expressions** there is much disagreement as to the correct verbs, but the following are generally accepted:

Six divided by three *is* two.   Seven minus two *is* five.
One fourth of twelve *is* three.   Five plus three *is* eight.
Five times two *are* ten.   Three and four *are* seven.

254 If the **infinitive** (194) refers to time coincident with that of the main verb or after it, use the present infinitive:

I intended *to sing* (not *to have sung*).

The **present infinitive** (194, 201) may be used with a verb in any tense, as follows:

He wishes *to meet* you.   He had wished *to meet* you.
He has wished *to meet* you.   He will wish *to meet* you.
He wished *to meet* you.   He will have wished *to meet* you.

When the **perfect infinitive** (194, 201) is used with a verb in the past tense or in the past perfect tense (188, 189) expressing *desire, hope,* or *duty,* it indicates that something interfered with the desire, hope, or duty:

She wished *to have seen* you. (She did not see you.)
I hoped *to have met* you. (I did not meet you.)

If the present infinitive is used after one of the verbs just mentioned, there is uncertainty:

He hoped *to meet* you. (Whether he did or not is uncertain.)

The use of the perfect infinitive (194, 201) after such verbs as *seem, appear,* and *know* shows that the incident denoted by the infinitive took place before the time indicated by the verb:

Bob seems *to have succeeded.*

255 It is incorrect to use a present participle to indicate action previous to that expressed by the main verb:

He has been away three days, *having left* (not *leaving*) last Monday.

Uses of Verbals

256 The **infinitive** (194, 225) has many uses:

1. **The infinitive used as a noun** (54, 58-5):
   a. **Subject of a verb** (91): *To win* is not easy.
   b. **Predicate nominative** (92): What he wants is *to win.*
   c. **Object of a verb:** He likes *to write.*
   d. **Nominative case in apposition with the subject** (96): His aim, *to succeed,* is commendable.
   e. **Objective case in apposition with object** (106): She has one great desire, *to succeed.*

Note: An infinitive may be used much as any other noun (382).

2. **The infinitive used as an adjective:** The house *to be sold* is new.
3. **The infinitive used as an adverb** (307): Mary came *to* see us.

Diagram—An infinitive used as subject:

To succeed is his intention.

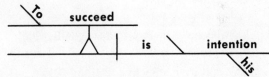

257 The **gerund** (54, 58-4, 195) has many noun uses, as follows:

1. **Subject of a verb:** *Stealing* is wrong.
2. **Object of verb:** I heard the *roaring* of the river.
3. **Object of preposition:** Do you object to my *smoking?*
4. **Apposition:** His work, *mining,* was dangerous.
5. **Predicate nominative:** His work is *painting* signs.

Diagram—A gerund used as **subject** (257-1) and having an object:

Running races is good exercise.

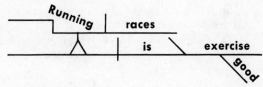

Diagram—A gerund used as **object** and having an object:
The boys dislike *picking* cotton.

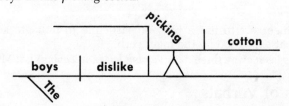

258 Some authorities say that a verbal may be called a pure noun when it has lost the verbal idea, when it may be pluralized, when it is preceded by an article and followed by a preposition, or when it is the name of an art, a course of study, or some form of exercise:

We attended the *wedding*.   The *rowing* of the boat was easy.

I know Bob's *failings*.   I am taking a course in *writing*.

259 A compound gerund is formed by placing a noun before a gerund: *mountain climbing*.

Note: The gerund is called **verbal noun** or **participial noun** (195). Some grammarians attempt to show a difference between the gerund and the verbal noun, but the difference is so slight as to be unimportant.

260 The **participle** is a verbal (193, 196) which is used as an adjective. It has the same uses as the regular adjective (267):

1. Attributive (268):

The *running* stream is beautiful.   The *broken* limb has fallen.

2. Predicate adjective (174-4, 269B), 280):

The game was *thrilling*.   The boy is *discouraged*.

3. Appositive adjective (269A):

The boy, *running* swiftly, soon disappeared.
The limb, *broken* by the wind, has fallen.

The participle ending in *ing* sometimes seems to be a pure adjective, and at other times it is thought of as a part of the verb in the progressive form (205):

The *gleaming* stars are beautiful. (resembles a pure **adjective**)
The stars, *gleaming* in the sky, are beautiful. (**regular participle**)
The stars are *gleaming* in the sky. (**part of the verb**)

The past participle (196) is sometimes used as an adjective and sometimes as the main part of the verb in the passive voice (180):

This drama, *written* by Thornton Wilder, is my favorite. (**adjective**)
This story was *written* by William Saroyan. (**part of the verb** in the passive voice)

Diagram—A participle (196) having an object:

John, *fearing defeat,* encouraged his comrades.

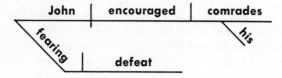

261 A noun or pronoun introducing a gerund is usually in the possessive case (111, 122):

He approved *Ann's* (not *Ann*) selling the book.
He did not like *my* (not *me*) going away.

This rule is not rigidly observed in conversation and informal writing.

Note: It sometimes requires close observation to distinguish the participle from the gerund:

We approved of the girl *playing* tennis. (**participle**)
We approved of the girl's *playing* tennis. (**gerund**)

262 A participial phrase (380-3) or a prepositional gerund phrase should have a substantive (45) which it can logically modify expressed in the sentence. When the substantive is omitted, the modifying phrase is said to be **dangling.** Dangling modifiers often result in absurdities. Be sure to give modifiers something to modify (435):

Running to the window, I saw a fire (not a *fire was seen*). (380-3) (The participial phrase *running to the window* modifies *I.* The fire was not running to the window.)
By working hard, we finished the task (not the *task was finished*). (380-4) (The prepositional phrase *by working hard,* which has a gerund as the object of the preposition, modifies *we.*)
Sitting in the moonlight, we enjoyed the music (not the *music was enjoyed*).

Note: A few set phrases, such as *generally speaking, considering everything,* are understood to modify the entire sentence, not any particular substantive in it.

Punctuation of participles and gerunds is very important. Note the use of the comma (478) in the examples just given. If a participial phrase begins the sentence, it is followed by a comma:

Singing gayly, the bird sat in the tree.

The absolute construction (95) is set off from the rest of the sentence by a comma or commas:

The game being ended, we went home.

Sometimes the word *being* is omitted from the absolute construction, but the comma is used:

The matter (being) *adjusted,* we felt relieved.

Nonrestrictive phrases (phrases not necessary to the meaning of the rest of the sentence) are set off by commas (478):

The man *sitting by the desk* is the principal. (**necessary**)

The old man, *sitting idly in the sun,* dreamed of other days. (**unnecessary**—comma used)

263   The **subject of an infinitive** (104, 194) is in the objective case:

We asked *him* to go. (*Him* is the subject of *to go.*)

Jack asked *her* to sing. (*Her* is the subject of *to sing.*)

264   In an **infinitive clause** (390) a predicate noun (92) or a predicate pronoun (140-2) used after *to be* is in the objective case to agree with the subject of the infinitive (105):

You thought us to be *them.*

They took me to be *her.*

265   If the infinitive *to be* has no subject, a predicate noun or a predicate pronoun following it is in the nominative case (105):

He was thought to be *I.*

I was believed to be *she.*

ADJECTIVES

266   An **adjective** is a modifier (7) which describes or limits a substantive (45). It may be a word or a group of words (7, 8, 9, 40):

We saw *beautiful* flowers.

Those flowers *on the desk* are roses. (*Those* is a simple modifier; the group is a phrase modifier, 380-1.)

Those boys *whom you saw* are students. (*Those* is a simple modifier; the group is a clause modifier, 397.)

The adjective is used effectively in painting word pictures—describing (524B). Note the effect of the added modifiers (7) in the illustration below:

Near the house stood a tree. (**unimpressive**)

Above the gray, old-fashioned, stone dwelling a tall, slender eucalyptus tree waved its feathery branches in the summer morning sunlight. (**vivid**)

267   Adjectives are used in three ways: **attributive, appositive,** and **predicate.**

268   The **attributive** use is that of the direct modifier, which precedes the substantive:

The man wore a *dark* suit.

Note: Adjectives in a series are usually separated by commas (484):
A *beautiful, tall, slender* pine stood near.

269A   The **appositive** follows directly the substantive it modifies:

The speaker, *tall* and *graceful,* soon won his audience. (The adjectives *tall* and *graceful* explain the appearance of the speaker. The adjective used appositively is set off by a comma or commas.)

269B   The **predicate** use of the adjective (174-4, 280) is to complete the meaning of the predicate and modify the subject:

The work was *difficult.*   Mountains are *beautiful.*

The predicate adjective is usually joined to the subject by a linking verb (175). (But see also 280.)

270   An adjective that describes a substantive (45) by expressing some quality belonging to it is called a **descriptive adjective:**

We saw *tall* trees.   They climbed *high* hills.

271   An adjective that points out a substantive or limits its meaning without expressing a quality is called a **limiting** or **definitive adjective:**

She sent us *those* flowers.   We saw *many* trees.

272   The **limiting** or **definitive adjectives** include **pronouns used as adjectives** (pronominal adjectives, both **indefinite** and **demonstrative,** 133, 134, 135), **numeral adjectives,** and the **articles.**

Pronouns in the possessive case (111, 112) are sometimes called **possessive adjectives** (126, 141):

John lost *his* book.

(The possessive adjective is also pronominal, 135.)

The **pronominal adjectives** (135), are given under the treatment of pronouns (126, 133, 134), but further illustrations of their uses are given here. Be sure to distinguish the pronoun use from the adjective use:

This book is a grammar. (**adjective**)
This is a book. (**pronoun, 133**)
Each should bring a book. (**pronoun**)
Each student should bring a book. (**adjective**)
We saw *her* at the show. (**pronoun, objective case**)
We saw *her* book on the desk. (**pronoun in the possessive case,** sometimes called a **possessive adjective, 126**)

273 Numeral adjectives indicate number. There are two classes which are generally used: **cardinal** and **ordinal.**

274 A **cardinal** number indicates how many elements there are in a set:

We saw *three* ships.

275 The **ordinal** gives the order in a sequence:

He won the *third* prize.

276 The adjectives *a, an,* and *the* are called **articles.**

277 *A* and *an* are called **indefinite articles** because they do not point out particular persons, places or things:

The hunter killed a deer and *an* eagle. (*An* is used before a word beginning with one of the following vowel sounds—*a, e, i, o, u.* Before a consonant, *a* is used.)

278 *The* is called the **definite article** because it points out a particular member of a class of persons, places, or things:

This is *the* book we need.

Note: *The* may also be used to indicate a generalized noun as representative of its class:

We have now studied *the* noun, *the* verb, and *the* adjective.

279 A **proper adjective** is derived from a proper noun or is a proper noun used as an adjective. It is generally written with a capital letter:

Although he is a *Chinese* student, he enjoys the *Colorado* climate.

280 A **predicate adjective** (269B) completes the verb and relates to the subject:

She looks *beautiful.*

Predicate adjectives are used with the linking verbs, such as *be* and *become* and such as the verbs of the senses, including *seems, appears, looks, tastes, feels, smells.* Avoid substituting an adverb (307) for an adjective after a linking verb (175):

The rose smells *sweet* (not *sweetly*).

He looks *bad* (not *badly*) since his illness.

Note: Predicate adjectives (and predicate nominatives, 92) may also occur after certain verbs (100) in the passive (180):

She was considered *beautiful.*

281 Many words commonly used as **pronouns** may be used as **modifying adjectives** (133, 134, 272):

That hat is made of fur.	I know *what* man you mean.
Which horse is yours?	*Any* boy can do *that* work.

Note: When the noun modified is omitted, each of these adjectives becomes a pronoun (133, 134, 272):

That is made of fur. (pronoun)

Comparison of Adjectives

282 Adjectives have **three degrees of comparison: positive, comparative, and superlative.**

283 The **positive degree** expresses a quality without comparison:

Joe is *tall.*

284 The **comparative degree** expresses a higher or lower degree than the positive when comparing two persons or things:

Kay is *taller* than Joan.   Joan is *less talkative* than Kay.

285 The **superlative degree** is the highest or lowest degree when comparing more than two persons or things:

Bob is the *tallest* boy in the club.   He is also the *least talkative* member.

286 Comparison is denoted in three ways:

1. By adding *er* or *est* to the positive degree: *large—larger—largest.*
2. By prefixing *more* and *most* or *less* and *least: graceful—more graceful—most graceful.*
3. By irregular inflection: *bad—worse—worst.*

Table of Comparison

Positive	Comparative	Superlative
much	more	most
long	longer	longest
beautiful	more beautiful	most beautiful

287 Use the comparative degree (284), not the superlative, in comparing two objects:

He is the *older* of the two boys.   She is the *more brilliant* of the two.

Note: The familiar expression, "Put your *best* foot forward," is considered correct.

288 Certain adjectives that express **absolute qualities** do not in the strictest sense admit of comparison, but many good writers compare them regularly while others use *more nearly* and *most nearly* as a compromise. The words *unique, perfect, square, straight, endless, dead, perpendicular* are in this group:

This is the *most* perfect rose. (questioned by some)
This is the *most nearly* perfect rose. (preferred by some)

However, when such words are not used with their usual literal meaning, they may be compared:

This is the *deadest* party I ever attended.

289   The comparative is used with *than* because only two things (whether individuals or groups) are involved:

The boys learn *faster* than the girls in school. (Two groups are compared.)

When comparing something with the rest of the class of things to which it belongs, use *other, else,* or some such word:

John is faster than any *other* boy in school. (John is compared with the rest of the boys.)

Usage

290   When a numeral adjective and a noun form a compound adjective, the singular form of the noun is used:

a thirty-*day* vacation, a five-*foot* fence.

291   When a plural adjective modifies a noun, as a rule the noun should be plural:

He rode ten *miles* (not *mile*).

292   Words such as *dozen, head, score, gross,* and *hundred* retain their singular form when preceded by an adjective expressing number:

He kept three *head* of horses.

293   *This* and *that* are the only adjectives inflected for number. *This* and *that* modify singular nouns: *these* and *those,* plural nouns:

I like *this* kind of book and *these* kinds of pencils.

She prefers *those* kinds of roses and *that* kind of aster.

294   *First* and *last,* when used with adjectives that express number, are placed before the adjectives to make the meaning clear:

Omit the *last* ten pages.

295   When two or more adjectives modify the same noun, clearness requires that the article *(a, an,* or *the)* be used before the first adjective only:

a blue, gray, and white bird. (one bird)

296   When two or more adjectives modify different nouns, one expressed and the others understood (241), the article is used before each adjective:

The large and *the* small house are mine. (two houses)

297   *Less* indicates amount; *fewer* denotes number:

Fewer than twenty boys played ball.

We hope for *less* rain this month.

298   The article *a* or *an* is not needed after *kind of* or *sort of:*

What *kind of* (not *kind of a*) book is that?

299   When two or more nouns are used to denote the same person or thing, the article should be used before the first noun only:

The teacher and preacher (one person) of the town was loved by everyone.

300   When nouns used together denote different persons or things, the article should be used before each noun:

The teacher and *the* minister are popular. (two persons)

301   In comparison use *so* instead of *as* after a negative such as *not:*

She is not *so* tall as Jane. (*So* is used in the negative statement.)

She is *as* tall as Mary. (*As* is used in the positive statement.)

302   Do not use an adjective for an adverb. Do not use *sure* for *surely, real* for *really, some* for *somewhat, different* for *differently:*

She *surely* (not *sure*) is beautiful.

He was *really* (not *real*) pleased to help.

Note: Some adverbs have two forms, one with *ly* and one like the adjective. The short form may be used in some sentences:

Drive *slow*.   He went *slowly* down the street

303   Remember that verbs of the senses, such as *smell, taste, feel, look,* are generally completed by adjectives, not adverbs:

She looks *beautiful*. (**adjective,** 174-4, 269B, 280)

304   After any words used as linking verbs (175), the adjective (269B, 280) form, not the adverb, should be used: *seem, become, appear, prove, remain, keep, stay.*

305   The verbs *turn* and *grow* used in the sense of *become* are followed by an adjective:

The leaves turn *red*.   The clouds grow *dark*.

306   Usually the suffix *-like* may be added to a noun to form an adjective: *homelike, lifelike, tigerlike.*

However, *-like* should not be added indiscriminately, to adjectives:

Doubtful: The flame was *bluelike*.

Better: The flame was *bluish*.

ADVERBS

307 An **adverb** may modify a **verb** (165-176), an **adjective** (266-280), another **adverb**, a **verbal** (193-196), a **preposition** (332-337), a **conjunction** (355-359), or occasionally a **substantive** (45, 58):

She sings *beautifully*. (*Beautifully* modifies the verb *sings*.)

He is a *very* great man. (*Very* modifies the adjective *great*.)

She smiled *rather* sadly. (*Rather* modifies the adverb *sadly*.)

By working *faithfully*, he won success. (*Faithfully* modifies the gerund *working*.)

The little girl, smiling *happily*, ran to meet her mother. (*Happily* modifies the participle *smiling*.)

She has learned to sing *beautifully*. (*Beautifully* modifies the infinitive to *sing*.)

He was *almost* under the tree. (*Almost* modifies the preposition *under*.)

She came *just* before I left. (*Just* modifies the conjunction *before*.)

Nearly all of them were lost. (*Nearly* modifies the indefinite pronoun *all*, see 134.)

The *newly* rich were not invited. (*Newly* modifies the noun equivalent *rich*; see 58. Compare 595.)

Note: Some grammarians say that an adverb may not modify the preposition alone, but may modify the entire phrase introduced by the preposition. They also say that an adverb may not modify a conjunction, but may modify the clause introduced by it. Therefore in the sentences above they would say that *almost* modifies the phrase *under the tree*, and that *just* modifies the clause *before I left*. Sometimes an adverb appears to modify an entire sentence and is therefore called a **sentence adverb**:

Evidently, he doesn't care what we think.

The adverb may be a single word, a phrase (8), or a clause (9):

The bird sang *joyfully*. (**word**)

The bird sang *with* joy. (**phrase**)

The bird sang *because it was happy*. (**clause**)

The addition of adverb modifiers gives life to expression, as is shown by the illustration below (see also 266):

The president spoke.

The new president spoke *briefly* but *enthusiastically* about the plans for the coming year.

Such expressions as *one by one, by and by, now and then,* and *little by little* are called **phrasal adverbs**.

308 According to their **use** in a sentence, adverbs may be grouped into three classes: **simple, interrogative,** and **conjunctive.**

309 A **simple adverb** is a simple modifier:

She spoke *kindly*.

310   An **interrogative adverb** is used in asking a question:
Where have you been?

311   A **conjunctive adverb** is used to connect independent clauses (357, 386). Some common conjunctive adverbs are: *accordingly, also, anyhow, besides, consequently, however, moreover, nevertheless, otherwise, still, then, therefore, yet:*
Joe did not like the course; *nevertheless,* he worked hard and made a good grade.
Joe did not like the course; he worked hard, *nevertheless,* and made a good grade.

A semicolon (469) is used between clauses joined by a conjunctive adverb whether the adverb begins the second clause, as in the first sentence above, or is used within it, as in the second sentence.

312   **Simple adverbs** are divided into classes: adverbs of **manner, time, place, degree,** and **number.**

313   **Adverbs of manner** indicate how the action takes place:
He walked *proudly.*

314   **Adverbs of time** indicate when the action takes place:
Fred left *yesterday.*

315   **Adverbs of place** indicate where the action takes place:
Some of my friends were *there.*

316   **Adverbs of degree** indicate how much:
She walked *rather* slowly.

317   **Adverbs of number** indicate order or how many times:
He arrived *first.*   He came only *once.*

318   Adverbs, like adjectives, have **three degrees of comparison** (282-286)—**positive, comparative,** and **superlative:** *slowly—more slowly—most slowly.* Generally, this is true only of adverbs of manner.

Usage

319   Do not use the adjective *most* for the adverb *almost* (569):
It seems that *almost* (not *most*) all the students are here. (See 307)

320   *Good* is an adjective; *well* is usually an adverb. Do not confuse these words:
He writes *well* (not *good*).   The apple tastes *good.* (See 280).

When it means "not sick," *well* is an adjective:
I am glad he is *well* again.

321   Do not use these as adverbial expressions: *anywheres, nowheres, somewheres, nowhere near, illy, muchly.*

322 When *very* or *too* modifies a past participle (196), it should be accompanied by another adverb, such as *greatly* or *much*.

John was very *much* excited.

Note: The adverb *very* is so much overused that it has little meaning. Use it seldom.

323 Do not use such words as *up* and *of* unnecessarily:

Let's *connect* (not *connect up*) these wires.

324 *Kind of* and *sort of* are better replaced by such adverbs as *rather* and *somewhat:*

She was *somewhat* (not *sort of*) sad.

325 Do not use *some* as an adverb in careful writing. Use *somewhat:*

He is *somewhat* better today.

326 *Thisaway* and *thataway* are dialectal forms:

Dialectal: The robbers went *thataway*.
Standard: The robbers went *that way*.

327 Do not use two negatives to express one negative idea; for example, do not use *not* with *hardly, scarcely, only, neither, never, no one, nobody, nothing, no,* or *none:*

There was *no one* at home.

As a rule, place *not* directly before the word it modifies:

Not every soldier can be a general.

Some seeming double negatives are correct:

She was not *unwilling* to help.   No *one* liked the play, *not* even Jane.

328 Use *from* after *different* and *differently* (351):

He thinks differently *from* (not *than*) you.

329 Do not use any word between the parts of an infinitive (194, 228) if it results in an awkward expression:

Awkward: He told me to *not* sell the book.
Correct: He told me *not* to sell the book.

330 Do not use the adjective *easy* for the adverb *easily:*

We can finish *easily* (not *easy*) by noon.

Note: Certain phrases, such as *take it easy, go easy,* are colloquially acceptable.

331 The position of adverbs is rather free in English, but sometimes the position of an adverb changes the meaning of a sentence:

He *only* seems interested in reading. (He is really not interested.)
He seems interested *only* in reading. (Reading is apparently his only interest.)

PREPOSITIONS

332   A **preposition** (42) is a word or a word group that shows the relation between its object (6) and some other word in the sentence:

The eagle soared *above* the peak. (*Above* is a preposition; *peak* is the object of the preposition. A preposition and its object form a prepositional phrase.

Note: A word ordinarily used as a preposition may be used as a simple adverb (307, 309) when it has no object, or it may become part of a verb:

We have met *before*. (**adverb**)

John arrived before dinner. (**preposition**)

Send *in* the applicant. Send the applicant *in*. He was sent *in*. (**adverb**)

333   Although prepositions are variously classified, it is sufficient to know three general classes: **simple, compound,** and **phrasal.**

334   A **simple preposition** is made up of one word: *by, for, in.*

335   A **compound preposition** is made up of two prepositions used as one: *from across, over against, from below.*

336   A **phrasal preposition** is any phrase used as a preposition (in general the phrasal preposition may be included with the compound): *in spite of, in accordance with, with regard to.*

337   Some of the words most frequently used as prepositions are *aboard, about, above, across, after, against, along, amid, among, around, at, before, behind, below, beneath, beside, between, beyond, by, down, during, except, for, from, from among, from between, from, under, in, into, of, off, on, out of, outside, over, round, round about, since, through, throughout, to, unto, under, underneath, up, upon, with,* and *within.*

338   A preposition and its object, with the modifiers of the object, form a phrase (8) which has the use of an **adjective** (266) if it modifies a noun or a pronoun, and the use of an **adverb** (307) if it modifies a verb, adjective, or an adverb:

The tree *in the park* is an oak. (**adjective phrase** modifying *tree*)

We walked *beside the river*. (**adverb phrase** modifying *walked*)

Note: Some authors feel that a prepositional phrase may be used as a noun (382). The following is an example:

At the door was where he left her.

Usage

339   Some authorities believe that many of the suggested preferences in the use of prepositions given in the following sections apply mostly to formal expression.

340 One may *agree to* a thing and *agree with* a person:
I *agree* to the plan.   You *agree* with me.

341 One may be *angry at* or *about* a thing and *angry with* a person:
I was *angry at* the discourtesy.   He was *angry with* me.

342 One *arrives in* a large city, *at* a small place:
He *arrived in* Chicago.   We *arrived at* the village.

343 *Besides* means *in addition to; beside* means *by the side of:*
He sat *beside* me.   There were two boys *besides* Henry.

344 *Between* refers to two; *among,* to more than two:
He divided the candy *between* the two boys.
He threw the gold *among* the five girls.

345 One is *accompanied by* a person, *with* a thing:
Mabel was *accompanied by* her mother.
The rain was *accompanied with* hail.

346 Do not use *inside of* for *within:*
He did not work *within* (not *inside of*) a week.

347 *Into* denotes entrance; *in* denotes location:
He jumped *into* the water.
He swam *in* the river.

348 One may die *of* disease, *from* exposure, or *by* violence:
He died *of* pneumonia.   She died *from* exposure.

349 *By* is the word to use after *follow* when referring to what follows:
The murderer was followed *by* a mob.

350 *Differ with* means *disagree in opinion; differ from* means *be unlike or dissimilar:*
I *differ with* you about the value of the painting.
The horses *differ from* each other in color.

351 *From* should be used with the adjective *different:*
This hat is different *from* (not *than*) that. (328)

352 One *parts from* a person, *with* a thing:
Romeo *parted from* Juliet.
The miser did not wish to *part with* his gold.

353 Do not use *in back of* for *behind:*
The garage is *behind* (not *in back of*) the house.

354 Do not use unnecessary words such as accept *of,* off *of,* remember *of,* where *at,* where *to.*

CONJUNCTIONS

355 A **conjunction** (43) connects words or groups of words; it may be a single word or a group of words:

Robert *and* James are here. (a single word connecting two words)

She came *while* you were away. (a single word connecting clauses)

The teachers *as well as* the students had a good time. (a group of words used as a conjunction)

Note: A conjunction such as that used in the last example is called a **phrasal conjunction.**

356 Although conjunctions have many classifications, it is sufficient for our purpose to note only the two general classes: **coordinate** and **subordinate.**

357 A **coordinate conjunction** connects two words, two phrases, or two clauses of equal rank:

Paul *and* Carl are here. (*And* connects two nouns.)

She liked to read *and* to write (not *writing*). (*And* connects two infinitives.)

The coordinate conjunctions in most general use include *and, but, for, nor.* The conjunctive adverbs such as *however, then, therefore,* and *still,* also connect independent clauses (311).

358 A **subordinate conjunction** connects two clauses of unequal rank; that is, it joins a dependent (subordinate) clause (387) to the independent clause (386) on which it depends:

I was here *before* you came.

Some of the subordinate conjunctions are *as, as if, because, before, if, since, that, till, unless, when, where, whether.*

359 Conjunctions which are used in pairs are called **correlatives** and include *both—and, either—or, neither—nor, not only—but also.*

Neither John *nor* I will be able to come.

Usage

360 Do not use *except* for *unless:*

We will play *unless* (not *except* or *without*) you object.

361 Do not use *without* for *that:*

I never meet her *that I do not* (not *without I*) think of her mother.

362 Do not use *like* for *as, as if,* or *that* in formal writing:

Walk *as* (not *like*) he told you.

It seems *that* (not *like*) he should help.

363 *And etc.* for *etc.* is incorrect. *Etc.* is an abbreviation of the Latin words *et cetera,* meaning *and so forth;* therefore, *and* is not needed.

364 *And, but* and *or* are used so frequently that a piece of writing may become overloaded with compound sentences. Learn to use other conjunctions also.

365 *And, or but,* and correlative conjunctions (359) should be used to join expressions that are parallel in form:

She liked to *stroll* in the woods *and to hear* (not *and hearing*) the birds sing.

366 Some grammarians insist that the relative (conjunctive pronoun) *which* should not be used to refer to an entire clause (161):

Doubtful: The roads were muddy, *which* caused me to be late.

Better: I was late because the roads were muddy.

367 When a subordinate conjunction (358) introduces two or more expressions of equal importance, the conjunction should usually be repeated before each clause to make the meaning clear:

He told me *that* he had won the prize and *that* his brother would return tomorrow.

368 *Nor* is used with *neither* or after some negative word:

He can neither read *nor* (not *or*) write.

He cannot dive, *nor* does he like to swim.

369 After verbs of *saying, thinking,* and *feeling,* do not use *as* to replace *that:*

I do not feel *that* (not *as*) I should go.

370 Do not use *where* for *that:*

I saw in the paper *that* (not *where*) the price of wheat had advanced.

371 Do not use *if* for *whether* in formal use:

I do not know *whether* (not *if*) he will come.

372 Each of a pair of correlatives (359) should be placed immediately before the word it connects:

I will eat *either* meat *or* fish. (not: I will *either* eat meat *or* fish.)

373 In clauses of purpose, do not use *so* for *so that* in formal use:

He worked hard so *that* he could pay his debts.

374 Use *when* to follow *scarcely* or *hardly;* use *than* to follow a comparative expression:

He had scarcely started *when* the accident happened.

He did better *than* I expected.

375 Use *that* before a clause which follows a verb of *saying, thinking,* or *feeling* when the verb is followed by an infinitive:

He studied hard, for he knew *that* to fail would be his ruin.

376 Do not omit *as* when it is necessary to complete a comparison:

Illogical: John is as tall, if not taller than you.

Logical: John is as tall as you, if not taller.

Three: *THE SENTENCE*

SENTENCE STRUCTURE AND ANALYSIS

377 A sentence must express a thought (1);* therefore it must have a subject and a predicate (3, 4) expressed or understood (5); and it may have modifiers (7) and independent elements (12).

378 In general, sentences are made up of **words, phrases** (8), and **clauses** (9). The classification of words has been given in Chapter 2 under *Parts of Speech.* Phrases and clauses are also variously classified.

379 A **phrase** is a group of related words used as a part of a sentence and not having a subject (3) or predicate (4). A phrase may be a modifier (7, 8), a connective (336, 355), or a substantive (45):

Ann came *with me.* (**modifier**)

To make a mistake is not necessarily disgraceful (**substantive**)

Note: The verb phrase (15, 39, 176, 380-Note) is not a modifier, a connective, nor a substantive.

380 **According to structure** there are four general classes of phrases: **prepositional, infinitive, participial,** and **gerund:**
1. A **prepositional phrase** includes a preposition (332, 337, 399C) and its object and modifiers, if any, of the object:
Burns lived *among the hills.*
2. An **infinitive phrase** includes an infinitive and its object or complement and modifiers, if any:
Byron liked *to write poetry.*
3. A **participial phrase** includes a participle and its object and modifiers, if any:
The girl, *smiling sweetly,* took her place.
4. A **gerund phrase** includes a gerund and its object and modifiers, if any:
Painting beautiful pictures is interesting work.

Note: The **verb phrase** is merely a phrasal verb—a verb made up of two or more words (39).

381 **According to their use** phrases are classified as follows: **noun** (substantive), **adjective,** and **adverb.**

382 A **noun phrase** may be used as a regular noun, with the exception that it is not used in the possessive case (111):
Playing tennis is delightful exercise. (This is a **gerund phrase,** 380-4, used as the subject. All gerunds are, of course, used as nouns, 195.)

* *Numbers in parentheses refer to sections of this book.*

The following are examples of other uses of gerunds as nouns:

My favorite exercise is *swimming*. (**predicate nominative,** 92)

Robert likes *swimming*. (**object of verb,** 98)

We talked about *swimming*. (**object of a preposition,** 102)

His work, *writing* stories, is very interesting. (**apposition with the subject,** 96, 97)

She likes her work, *teaching* music. (**apposition with object of verb**)

The infinitive phrase (380-2) has the following uses as a noun:

To try is noble. (**subject**)

I like *to swim*. (**direct object**)

His desire is *to succeed*. (**predicate nominative**)

His aim, *to succeed*, is worthy. (**apposition with subject**)

I dread my task, *to sell tickets*. (**apposition with object of verb**)

He spoke of his duty, *to work*. (**apposition with object of preposition**)

The prepositional phrase (380-1, 338) is not regularly used as a noun, but some writers give the following as an example:

Over the fence is out.

Note: The participial phrase (380-3) is used as an adjective and not as a noun; but the gerund is in reality a form of participle used as a noun and is sometimes called **verbal noun** or **participial noun** (54, 195).

383   An **adjective phrase** is a phrase used as an adjective (40, 266-280, 399C). The prepositional (380-1), the infinitive phrase (380-2), or the participial phrase (380-3) may be used as an adjective:

The house *on the hill* is white. (**prepositional phrase** used as an adjective to modify *house*)

Evelyn has a great deal of work *to do*. (**infinitive phrase** used as an adjective to modify *work*)

The boy *holding the bat* is Harold. (**participial phrase** used as an adjective to modify *boy*)

384   An **adverb phrase** is a phrase used as an adverb (41, 307-317, 399C). Phrases used as adverbs are generally either prepositional or infinitive:

Helen came *with Mary*. (**prepositional phrase** used as an adverb to modify *came*)

The boys came *to work*. (**infinitive phrase** used as an adverb to modify *came*)

Note: A phrase may sometimes be either adjective or adverb:

He saw a book *on the table*.

385   A **clause** is a group of words which contains a subject (3) and a predicate (4). It is usually considered a part of a sentence; but when

it is capable of standing alone, it is equivalent to a simple sentence
(21). Words are sometimes properly omitted from the clause (10):

The officer said, "*Stop.*" (*You,* the **subject,** is here **omitted.**)

Mary is the girl *who wrote the letter.*

Clauses as related to the sentence are classified as **independent** (also
called **principal clause,** or **main clause**) and **dependent** (**subordinate**).

386 The **independent clause** is one which could make complete sense
if left standing alone and which is grammatically independent.

Robert delivers papers before he comes to school. (The clause *Robert
delivers papers* could stand alone, for it expresses a complete thought.)

387 A **dependent** (subordinate) **clause** is used as a part of speech in a
sentence and usually does not make sense when standing alone:

Robert delivers papers *before he comes to school.* (The clause *before
he comes to school* does not make complete sense when standing alone;
it is also used as an adverb modifying the verb in the main clause.)

388 A **dependent clause** may be used as a **noun,** an **adjective,** or an
adverb. The **noun clause** may be used in a variety of ways. These
uses are illustrated in sections 389-396. **Adjective clauses** and **adverb
clauses** are explained in sections 397 and 398.

Noun Clause

389 Noun clause used as subject (3) of the sentence:

What he thought seemed important to her.

390 Noun clause used as direct object of a verb (6):

Don said *that he tried.*

Note: An infinitive (194) construction which sometimes replaces a
that clause is sometimes called an **infinitive clause:**

John asked *me to stay.* (This is equivalent to *John asked that I should
stay;* therefore *me to stay* is a noun clause, of which *me* is the subject—the subject of an infinitive is always in the objective case—and
to stay is the predicate. *Me to stay* is the direct object of *asked.*)

391 Noun clause used as object of a preposition (102):

We talked about *what we would do.*

392 Noun clause used as predicate nominative (92):

The fact is *that he won the prize.*

393 Noun clause used in apposition (96) with the subject:

The report *that he won* is correct.

394 Noun clause used in apposition (97) with object of a verb:

You made the statement *that he won.*

395   Noun clause used in apposition with object of a preposition:
We thought of his answer, "*I do not care.*"

396   Noun clause used in apposition (96) with the predicate nominative:
The clearest evidence is the fact *that he won.*

Adjective Clause

397   An **adjective clause** is a clause used as an adjective (266, 400). The adjective clause may be introduced by a relative pronoun (130), a relative adverb (such as *where, when, while, why*) or a subordinate conjunction (358). The relative adverbs are also classed as subordinate conjunctions, but when introducing adjective clauses, they have antecedents. In some instances, the word which connects the clause is omitted:

This is the book *that I bought.* (adjective clause, modifying *book,* introduced by the pronoun *that*)

That is the place *where we saw him.* (adjective clause, modifying *place,* introduced by the relative adverb *where*)

Is that the girl *we met yesterday?* (adjective clause omitting the introductory pronoun)

Whether the introductory word is expressed or not, it must be considered as a part of the clause. The omitted word in the last example is *whom,* and it must be considered the object of *met.*

Adverb Clause

398   An **adverb clause** is a clause used as an adverb (307-317, 400). The adverb clause is introduced by a subordinate conjunction (358):

When we had finished our difficult task, we drove through the park. (The subordinate conjunction *when* introduces the adverb clause which modifies the verb *drove.*)

The adverb clause which stands at the beginning of a sentence is followed by a comma (476) unless it is very short. A comma is usually not used when the main clause (386) stands first:

We drove through the park *when we had finished our difficult task.*
We stayed at home *because the weather was unpleasant.* (The subordinate conjunction *because* introduces the adverb clause which modifies the verb *stayed.*)

SENTENCE FORM

399   A sentence (1, 377) must have a subject and a predicate (2) and it may have other parts, such as objects, complements, and modifiers of all types (1-20). As to form, a sentence may be classified as **simple** (21), **compound** (22), **complex** (23), and **compound-complex** (402). The **simple sentence** must have **but one** independent clause (386). The subject (3) or the predicate (4) or both (19) may be compound; and it may contain any number of phrases, but no dependent clause (387):

> The man at the window sent a ticket for John. (This simple sentence contains two phrases.)

> Jane and Bess gathered the roses and daisies and arranged them in the vases. (This simple sentence contains a compound subject, a compound predicate, a compound direct object, and one phrase.)

Although there are certain parts (2) necessary to every sentence, all sentences are made up of words and groups of words. We have noted the classification of words as parts of speech (36-50), (51-376), and the classification of groups of words as phrases and clauses (379-398). In the study of the relationships of the parts of the sentence, there are three methods used by grammarians: **parsing, analyzing,** and **diagraming.**

399A **Parsing a word** is naming the part of speech (36-50) to which it belongs, its modifications, and its construction in the sentence:

> Mary paints beautiful pictures.

Mary is a proper noun (52), feminine gender (62), third person (69), singular number (71), nominative case (91), subject of the verb *paints*.

Paints is a regular transitive verb (166, 169), indicative mood (182), present tense (186), active voice (179), third person (69), singular number (71) to agree (192) with its subject *Mary*.

Beautiful is a descriptive adjective (270), positive degree (283), and modifies the noun *pictures*.

P ctures is a common noun (53), neuter gender (63), third person (69), plural number (72), objective case (98), object of the verb *paints*.

399B **Analyzing a sentence** is giving the relation of the parts of the sentence to each other:

> The little girl liked the roses in the garden.

This is a simple declarative sentence (21, 25).

The little girl is the complete subject (14); *girl* is the simple subject (13); *the* and *little* are adjectives modifying *girl. Liked the roses in the garden* is the complete predicate (16); *liked,* the simple predicate (15), is completed by the object *roses* (98). The object (6) is modified by the adjective *the* and the adjective phrase (383) *in the garden.*

399C **Diagraming** is giving a picture of word relationships. Other diagrams of the simple sentence are given under 4, 6, 7, 19, 92, 96, 101, 174, 256, 257, and 260.

Diagram—*A simple sentence with a prepositional phrase* (380) *used as an adjective* (383):

The book *on the desk* is blue.

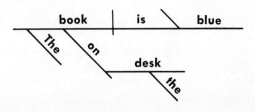

Diagram—*A simple sentence* (21) *with a prepositional phrase used as an adverb* (384):

A dog ran *under the fence.*

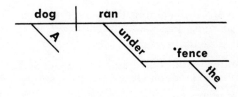

400 A **complex sentence** (23) has **but one** independent clause (386) and **one or more** dependent clauses (387):

Ruth left *when I arrived.* (*Ruth left* is an **independent clause.** *When I arrived* is a **dependent clause** which modifies the verb *left* as an adverb, 398.)

This is the boy *who wrote the story that won the prize.* (*This is the boy* is an **independent clause.** *Who wrote the story* is a **dependent clause** which modifies the noun *boy* as an adjective, 397. *That won the prize* is a **dependent clause** that modifies *story* as an adjective.)

The analysis of a complex sentence is similar to that of the simple sentence:

Bob saw the boy who wrote the story.

This is a complex sentence. *Bob saw the boy* is the main, or independent, clause, of which *Bob* is the subject, *saw* is the verb, and *boy* is the direct object. The dependent clause is *who wrote the story; who* is the subject of the dependent clause, *wrote* is the verb, and *story* is the direct object. The dependent clause is an adjective (397), and it modifies the noun *boy.*

Diagram—*A complex sentence with an adjective clause* (397) *intro-duced by a relative pronoun* (130) *used as object:*

I saw the horse *which you bought.*

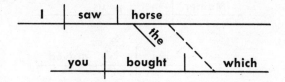

Diagram—*A complex sentence with an adjective clause introduced by a relative pronoun* (130) *used as subject:*

The girl *who sat beside me* is my cousin.

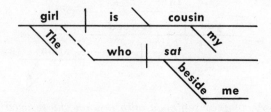

Diagram—*A complex sentence with an adjective clause introduced by a relative adverb* (397):

That is the place *where we saw the deer.*

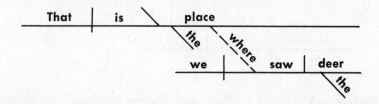

Diagram—*A complex sentence with an adverb clause* (398) *intro-duced by the subordinate conjunction* (358) *if:*

She will win *if we help her.*

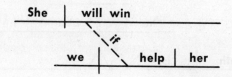

Diagram—A complex sentence with an adverb clause introduced by the subordinate conjunction when (358):

Mother met us *when we arrived.*

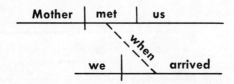

Diagram—A complex sentence with a noun clause used as subject (389):

That you succeed is the truth.

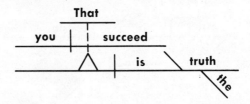

Diagram—A complex sentence with a noun clause used as the object of a verb (390):

My brother said *that he had won the prize.*

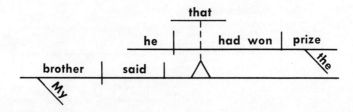

Diagram—A complex sentence with a noun clause used as subjective complement, or predicate nominative (392):

The truth is *that he bought the house.*

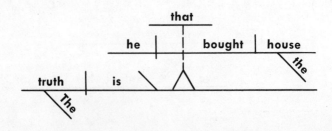

401 A **compound sentence** (22) has **two or more** independent clauses (386) joined by conjunctions (355-359) or by punctuation (468, 474) or by both:

> The little girl went to school, but her brother stayed at home.
> The little girl went to school; her brother stayed at home.

When there are no other commas used in a compound sentence, a comma is placed before the conjunction (474). When the conjunction is not used, as in the second example, a semicolon (468) separates the clauses. The two clauses of the sentence, being independent (386), might stand alone as sentences. But when an independent clause is changed into a sentence, it ceases to be a clause, for a clause is a part of a sentence:

> The little girl went to school. Her brother stayed at home. (two simple sentences)

The compound sentence is analyzed the same as simple sentences except that the connecting words are mentioned. Every independent clause is practically equivalent to a simple sentence, and a compound sentence may have any number of independent clauses:

> The little girl went to school; her brother stayed at home; her father went to his office. (three clauses connected by semicolons, 468)

Diagram—A compound sentence:

John goes to college, but Mary stays at home.

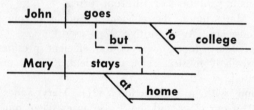

402 If either independent clause of a compound sentence has a subordinate clause (387), the sentence is called **compound-complex,** or **complex-compound:**

> When Henry lost the race, he was disappointed; but he was not discouraged.

Diagram—A compound-complex sentence:

He lost the knife that he bought, but he may find it.

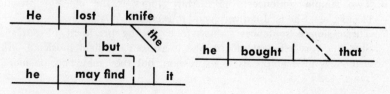

SENTENCE STYLE

403   Sentences are also classified as to the arrangement of their material as **periodic, loose,** and **balanced.**

404   A **periodic sentence** is one in which the main thought is not given until the end of the sentence is reached. It lends emphasis:

Today, as never before in the history of the world, we need leadership.

(A compound sentence as a whole cannot be periodic, but its parts may be periodic.)

405   The **loose sentence** gives the main thought and then adds details. It is the rambling type much used in conversation:

Lancelot returned with Guinevere in the spring when the flowers were in bloom and the world seemed full of gladness.

406   The **balanced sentence** has two parts which are similar in construction. The thought in the two parts may be either in agreement or contrast:

He was always industrious, but he was never successful.

Variety

407   **Variety in Sentence Structure.** One form of sentence may be just as effective as another, but any form becomes monotonous when it is used too frequently. Valuable practice can be had by expressing similar ideas in sentences of different form:

1. **Simple:** Mary Jones, the efficient president of our class, is an excellent musician. (An appositive, 97, is used.)
2. **Complex:** Mary Jones, who is the efficient president of our class, is an excellent musician. (A dependent, 387, nonrestrictive clause, 478, is used.)
3. **Compound with a conjunction** (401): Mary Jones is the efficient president of our class, and she is also an excellent musician. (A comma, 474, precedes the conjunction.)
4. **Compound without a conjunction** (401): Mary Jones is the efficient president of our class; she is also an excellent musician. (A semicolon, 468, separates the independent clauses.)
5. **Compound-complex** (402): Mary Jones, who is the president of our class, is a very efficient officer; and she is also an excellent musician. (For punctuation, see 470, 478.)
6. **Two simple sentences** (399): Mary Jones is the efficient president of our class. She is also a very good musician.
7. **Three simple sentences:** Mary Jones is the president of our class. She is a very efficient officer. She is also an excellent musician. (Short sentences give emphasis to expression, but they may become monotonous, 433.)

408 Variety in Word Groups. Through variety in word groups, sentences may be kept free from monotony:

1. **Phrase** (380-3): *Completing the work,* the men went home.
2. **Clause** (387): The men *who completed the work* went home.
3. **Clause** (398): *When the men completed the work,* they went home.
4. **Phrase** (380-3): *Having completed the work,* the men went home.
5. **Absolute construction** (95): *The work being completed,* the men went home.
6. **Absolute construction** (95): *The work completed,* the men went home.
7. **Gerund** (54, 195): *After completing the work,* the men went home.

Note: The use of the participial phrase (380-3) to replace the adjective clause (397) lends economy and often strength:

The man *standing beside the gate* is an officer. (**phrase**)

The man *who is standing beside the gate* is an officer. (**clause**)

409 Variety in Arrangement. In the arrangement of the material in sentences, there should be variety as to the place of emphasis. The periodic sentence (404) gives emphasis to the important idea in a sentence, but it should not be used to the exclusion of the loose sentence (405).

Yesterday afternoon about four o'clock my friend met with a serious accident. (**periodic sentence**)

My friend met with a serious accident yesterday afternoon about four o'clock. (**loose sentence**)

410 Variety in Length. The length of sentences should be varied. Short sentences become tiresome when used to excess, and a continuation of long sentences has a tendency to confuse the reader.

411 Variety of Beginning. Sentences which begin in the natural order (28A) of subject first may become as tiresome as any other oft-repeated sentence; therefore variety of beginning is necessary in making expression attractive. The following beginnings are suggestive of variety:

412 A sentence may begin with a prepositional phrase (380-1):

In those days men loved dangerous adventure.

413 A sentence may begin with a participial phrase (380-3):

Hoping to reach home before the storm, the rider urged his horse forward.

The day being beautiful, we played tennis. (**absolute, 95**)

414 A sentence may begin with an adverb (307):

Silently and *sadly* the old man turned away.

A sentence may begin with an adjective (266):

Beautiful as the trees were, they were cut down for the building.

415 A sentence may begin with a direct object of a verb (93):
Friends and *enemies* alike he betrayed in order that he might gain wealth.

416 A sentence may begin with a dependent clause (387):
That you are in earnest will help your cause. (**noun,** 389)
When the time comes, we will act. (**adverb,** 398)

417 A sentence may begin with a verb (39) or verbal (193):
Work hard if you wish to succeed.
To succeed is the desire of nearly everyone. (**infinitive phrase,** 380-2)
Helping others gives real joy. (**gerund phrase,** 380-4)

Effectiveness

418 **Effective Sentences.** An effective sentence must maintain **unity, coherence,** and **emphasis.**

419 **Unity** requires that the sentence must express a connected thought. The relationship of thoughts must be clearly shown:
Poor: Fred Smith visited me last summer, and he once lived in England.
Better: Fred Smith, who visited me last summer, once lived in England.

420 **Coherence** requires that the connection between different parts of the sentence be made perfectly clear:
Confusing: Ruth returned the book which she had borrowed last week this afternoon.
Clear: This afternoon Ruth returned the book which she had borrowed last week.

421 **Emphasis,** or force, is given the main ideas in a sentence by placing them properly in the positions of greatest emphasis—the beginning and the close. Force is given by arranging ideas in order of climax, by repetition of words or sounds, by the use of figures of speech (574), by the addition of modifiers (266, 307), through conciseness of expression, and through variety (407-417):

421A Emphasis gained by **position:**
Poor. After a long search they found the lost child finally in the woods.
Better: After a long search in the woods they found the lost child.

421B Emphasis gained by **climax:**
Flood has brought to these people *hunger, disease, death.* (See anticlimax, 441.)

421C Emphasis gained by **repetition:**
Mr. Smith is a man who is *true—true* to friends, *true* to enemies, *true* to himself.

Note: The repetition of the same beginning letter or sound, called *alliteration,* is used effectively in advertising: *w*atch, *w*ait, *w*in.

421D   Emphasis gained by **figures of speech:**
1. **Simile** (574A): The oak stood *like a sentinel.*
2. **Metaphor** (574B): The rose is *queen* of all flowers.
3. **Personification** (574D): The trees *laughed* in the June sunlight.
4. **Hyperbole** (574E): He gave a *thousand* excuses for his failure.

421E   Emphasis gained by **addition of modifiers** (266, 307):
He is a *handsome, intelligent, ambitious* young man.

421F   More **concise expression** sometimes adds force. Conciseness may be gained by changing form:
1. An appositive (97) may be substituted for a sentence:
Fred Smith addressed the meeting. *He is our president.*
Fred Smith, *our president,* addressed the meeting.

2. A participial phrase (383) may replace a clause (385):
The man *who is standing near the desk* is the president.
The man *standing near the desk* is the president.

The participial phrase also may be used to replace a sentence:
The beautiful building was destroyed by fire. *It was completed only a year ago.*
The beautiful building, *completed only a year ago,* was destroyed by fire.

3. A noun clause (389-396) may replace a sentence:
George is ambitious. *That fact is evident.*
That George is ambitious is evident.

4. A gerund may make a sentence more concise (195, 257):
It is my ambition to achieve worthy success.
The *achieving* of worthy success is my ambition.

5. An infinitive may make a sentence more concise (194, 256):
That I may win worthy success is my ambition.
To win worthy success is my ambition.

Structure and Style

422   **Confusing Reference.** A sentence may be faulty because a pronoun is placed where it may refer to more than one word: **There should be no uncertainty as to what word is the antecedent** (124) **of a pronoun.**

423   Confusing reference of the relative pronoun:

Confusing: She left the book on the table which she had just bought from the publisher. (The *which* seems to refer to *table,* though it should refer to *book.*)

Clear: She left on the table the book which she had just bought from the publisher. (The *which* clearly refers to *book.*)

424 Confusing reference of the personal pronoun:

    Confusing: Harry told Fred that he would become a great musiciar (It is not clear whether *he* refers to *Harry* or to *Fred.*)

    Clear: Harry said to Fred, "You will become a great musician. Or, Harry said to Fred, "I will become a great mu sician."

425 An indefinite antecedent (124) of the pronoun:

    Confusing: She asked me to help her, but I paid no attention to it (The *it* has nothing definite to refer to.)

    Clear: She made a request that I help her, but I paid no atten tion to it. (The antecedent is *request.*)

426 As a rule avoid using *which* to refer to a clause:

    Ineffective: My uncle came to see me, which pleased me greatly. (See 161, 366.)

    Better: I was pleased because my uncle came to see me.

427 Do not use *them* for *those:*

I think *those* (not *them*) roses are lovely.

Do not use *they* with indefinite reference (164):

People (not *They*) say he is honest.

428A **Unrelated Ideas.** Unrelated ideas should not be placed in the same sentence:

    Disconnected: Fred won the race, and he likes chocolate candy.

428B **Comma Blunder.** Two independent clauses (386) not joined by a conjunction should not be separated by a comma unless they are very short or make up a series (475). They should be separated by a semicolon (468) or be written as two sentences:

    Incorrect: We spent the summer in Colorado, we had a good time.

    Correct: We spent the summer in Colorado; we had a good time.

    Correct: We spent the summer in Colorado, and we had a good time.

    Correct: We spent the summer in Colorado. We had a good time.

429 **Run-On Blunder.** A serious writing error is the run-on sentence in which two sentences are written as one without a period or a semi-colon (33):

    Incorrect: We rambled through the woods all day we did not reach home till late.

    Correct. We rambled through the woods all day. We did not reach home till late.

430 **Period Fault.** Through the misuse of the period, students some-times write fragments for sentences:

Incorrect: We returned home. Hoping to have another picnic soon. (A participial phrase, 380-3, is written as a sentence.)
Correct: We returned home, hoping to have another picnic soon.
Incorrect: They liked all kinds of games. Especially football.
Correct: They liked all kinds of games, especially football.
Incorrect: We had a good time. When we were in Colorado. (A dependent clause, 387, is written as a sentence.)
Correct: We had a good time when we were in Colorado.

Note: Mature professional writers occasionally use the fragment very effectively in their work, but the young writer should construct complete sentences.

431   And-And Construction. It sounds childish to join many sentences by *and* as if all the ideas were of equal rank:

Childish: We finished our work, and we went fishing, and we had a good time.
Improved: After we had finished our work, we went fishing and had a good time.

432   Omission of Necessary Words.

432A   Subject of Sentence Omitted. The subject should be expressed in a declarative sentence (25) in order to make the meaning clear (31):

Faulty: Went to the football game yesterday.
Correct: I went to the football game yesterday.

In the imperative sentence (26) the subject is correctly omitted:

Correct: Lend me your book.

432B   Subject of Dependent Clause Omitted:

Not Clear: When in Chicago, my father sent me a watch.
Correct: When I was in Chicago, my father sent me a watch.
Not Clear: When ten years old, his mother died.
Correct: When he was ten years old, his mother died.

In elliptical sentences (5) the omission of words gives strength rather than weakness:

Welcome. (*You are* welcome.)
Where have I been? At school. (*I have been* at school.)
Do you like Shakespeare's plays? Yes. (Yes, *I like Shakespeare's plays.*)

433   Primer Sentences. Some students fall into the habit of writing monotonous short sentences like those in a primer:

Childish: We went to town. We stayed all day. We came home. We were tired.
Better: After we had spent the day in town, we came home tired.

Note: Short sentences of the mature type may at times be used effectively for emphasis:

He planned. He worked. He succeeded.

434 Parallel Structure. Parallel thoughts should be expressed in terms which are grammatically parallel:

Faulty: *Swimming* is more enjoyable than *to row.* (One is a gerund and the other is an infinitive.)

Better: *Swimming* is more enjoyable than *rowing.* (Both are gerunds, 195.)

Better: *To swim* is more enjoyable than *to row.* (Both are infinitives, 194.)

435 Dangling Modifiers. Modifiers should not be left dangling—with nothing to modify (262). A participial phrase (380-3), or a prepositional phrase (380-1) at the beginning of a sentence relates to the subject of that sentence. A participial phrase at the beginning of a sentence is followed by a comma:

Faulty: On entering the door, the picture is seen. (There is nothing for the phrase to modify; the *picture* does not do the *entering.*)

Clear: On entering the door, one may see the picture. (The introductory prepositional phrase which contains a gerund modifies *one.*)

Faulty: Walking down the street, the beautiful building was admired. (The *building* did no walking.)

Clear: Walking down the street, we admired the beautiful building.

435A Misplaced Modifiers. Modifiers—whether they are words (331), phrases, or clauses—should be so placed that their meaning is clear (423):

Confusing: She *almost* spent a hundred dollars.

Clear: She spent *almost* a hundred dollars.

Confusing: We saw a man on a horse with a wooden leg.

Clear: We saw a man with a wooden leg on a horse.

Confusing: Jane saw a hat in a window which she liked. (423)

Clear: Jane saw in a window a hat which she liked.

Shifts in Structure

436 Avoid needless shifts in **person:**

One must work if *one* (not *you*) would succeed.

437 Avoid needless shifts in **number:**

One should do *one's* (not *their*) duty.

438 Avoid needless shifts in **voice** (245, 246):
As we went up the path, *we saw a snake* (not *a snake was seen*).

439 Avoid needless shifts in **tense**:
The hunter went into the woods and there he *saw* (not *sees*) a deer.

440 Avoid needless shifts in **subject**:
Ted's letters are interesting, for *they are cleverly written* (not *he is a clever boy*).

441 Anticlimax. The sentence may lose effectiveness from anticlimax, the reverse of climax (421B), arranging ideas in the order of descending importance:
Flood has brought to these people *death, hunger, disease.*

442 Effective Repetition. Repetition of words may strengthen or weaken composition, depending upon whether important or trivial ideas are repeated.

443 A sentence may be strengthened by repetition of important words or ideas (421C).

444 Monotonous Repetition. Avoid the careless repetition of words:
Monotonous: *Autumn* is the most *enjoyable* time of year, for it is in *autumn* that the weather is most *enjoyable.*
Improved: Autumn is the most enjoyable time of the year, for it is the season when the weather is most pleasant.

444A Wordiness. A sentence may lose some of its effectiveness through wordiness—lack of economy in the use of words:
Lack of economy: He spoke in a very enthusiastic manner to the boys and girls of the high school about the wonderful opportunities of the future which lay ahead of them.
More concise: He spoke with enthusiasm to the high-school students about the opportunities of the future.

Redundancy denotes the use of unnecessary words:
Joe, *he* works fast.   This *here* book is good.

Tautology is the needless repetition of an idea in different words:
She is a widow *woman.*   It is an ancient, *old* castle.

444B Artificial Expression. A sentence may lose in strength because of artificial expression:
Artificial: A vast concourse of those amicably inclined toward him assembled to do him honor on his natal day.
Natural: Many of his friends came to celebrate his birthday.

Four: MECHANICS OF COMPOSITION

CAPITALIZATION

445 Every sentence except a short parenthetical sentence within another should begin with a capital letter:

The day was beautiful.

Mary left yesterday (*she* had been here a week) for New York City.

446 In most poetry every line begins with a capital:

"*Poems* are made by fools like me,

But only God can make a tree."

Some modern poets do not follow this rule.

447 The first word of a direct quotation should begin with a capital letter:

The girl said, "*Wait* for me."

448 The first word of a formal statement or resolution following introductory italicized words should be capitalized:

Resolved, That the world is growing better.

449 Every proper noun (52)* and every adjective derived from a proper noun (279) should be capitalized: *Boston, John Smith, French, American.*

450 The names of the days of the week, special holidays, and the names of the months should be capitalized: *Sunday, June.*

451 Names of the seasons are not capitalized ordinarily:

I like *summer* better than *winter.*

452 Names of particular associations and proper names resulting from membership in these associations should be capitalized: *Republican Party, Democrat, Methodist, Garden Club.*

Note: Classes, schools, and colleges are capitalized when they refer to the particular:

John is a senior in Brown *College;* he attended Oak *High School.*

The *Junior Class* invited Miss Smith to speak.

The use of capitals seems to be optional in some instances in which class names are used to refer to particular classes:

The *Juniors* (or *juniors*) have come.

453 Some abbreviations, such as the following, are usually written with capitals: *A.D., B.C., No., R.R.*

Abbreviations of titles and organizations are capitalized: *Dr., Ph.D., A.A.A., A.C.S.*

* *Numbers in parentheses refer to sections of this book.*

454 Important historical events and documents should be capitalized: *Battle of Hastings, World War II, the Declaration of Independence.*

School subjects, unless derived from proper names, are not capitalized except in numbered courses:
We study *history* and *English.* I'll take *Science 102* next year.

455 The words *east, west, north,* and *south* are capitalized when they mean particular sections of the country, but they are not capitalized when they mean directions:
He came from the *South.* (a **section of the country**)
He went *south* from town. (a **direction**)

The compounds of these words follow the same rule:
He lives in the great *Northwest.*
Is Hutchinson *northwest* of Wichita?

456 Nouns and personal pronouns (127) referring to God or to Christ are capitalized; but some writers do not capitalize the personal pronoun when its antecedent (124) is expressed:
I know *He* is the *Lord.*   Jesus loves *his* friends.

457 Names for the Bible and parts of the Bible should begin with capital letters:
Bible, the Scriptures, Old Testament, Deuteronomy. (Do not italicize these words.)

458 The first, last, and important words in the titles of books, literary articles, pictures, musical compositions, chapters of books, poems, plays, stories, newspapers, and magazines should begin with capitals. Prepositions, articles, and conjunctions are usually not capitalized unless they begin the title, but prepositions of four or more letters often are capitalized. If an article begins the title of a magazine or newspaper, it is not capitalized unless it begins a sentence:
"Ode on a Grecian Urn"   He reads the New York *Times.*

459 The words *I* and *O* are always capitalized.

460 The initials of a person's name should be capitals.

461 Titles used with proper names should be capitalized:
We think that *Captain Smith* would make a good school *principal,* but he prefers to be a *captain.*
He saw *Principal* John Moore at the meeting of *principals and superintendents.*

462 When a title is used as a proper noun referring to a particular person, it is correct to capitalize it:
The *President* of the United States spoke today.
Ann went with *Mother* and me to see her *mother.*

Note: There is much disagreement among authorities as to the application of this rule. It seems the preference to capitalize the word *president* when it refers to the President of the United States whether it refers to a particular man or not, but not to capitalize it, except when used with a name, for other persons, even with particular reference. Capitalization of such a term as *mother, father, uncle, sister,* or *cousin,* when it refers to a particular person, is considered optional by most writers; but some consider the use of the capital obligatory when the title is used in direct address. If, however, a possessive immediately precedes such a term, no capital is used. The following are correct:

I went with *Mother* to Chicago.

I went with *my mother* to Chicago.

Will you help me, *Father,* with this work?

I went with *my father* to New Orleans.

463 Common nouns are capitalized when they are strongly personified:

Come, lovely *Autumn,* and make us glad.

464 A common noun, such as *river, mountain, park, lake, gulf, ocean, street, avenue, hotel, church, school, club, society,* or *company,* is properly capitalized when it becomes a part of a particular name:

Is Lowell *School* near Belmont *Park?*

Does Clifton *Avenue* cross Maple *Street?*

Note: There is lack of agreement as to the application of this rule. Some good authorities capitalize only the first word in names of which these words are part. Many newspapers use the form given below; the schools seem to prefer the form already illustrated:

Is Lowell *school* near Belmont *park?*

Does Clifton *avenue* cross Maple *street?*

If the common noun precedes the particular name, it is capitalized even in the newspapers:

He lives near *Lake* Erie.

PUNCTUATION — Period

465 A period should be placed at the end of every declarative (25) and every imperative (26) sentence unless it is used as an exclamatory (28) sentence or in a sentence used parenthetically within another sentence (445). An elliptical expression (5, 432) used as a substitute for a sentence is followed by a period or other end punctuation:

Jean went to Europe last summer. (**declarative**)

Let me see your new book. (**imperative**)

Fred Jones (he is president of our class) will arrange the program. (**parenthetical sentence** with no capital, 445, and no period)

Yes. (**elliptical**)

Note: The polite request disguised as a question, so frequent in letters, is generally followed by a period, not a question mark (506):

Will you please send your latest catalog.

466   Use periods after initials and most abbreviations (see also 514A): *A.D., B.C., C.O.D., No., Geo. F. Smith, LL.D.*

There are many exceptions, such as *IQ, DDT.* Abbreviations of many organization names omit periods: *WAFS, WAVES;* or may be written either way: *Y.M.C.A.* or *YMCA, USMC* or *U.S.M.C.*

Consult the dictionary as a guide to the handling of abbreviations. Do not use a period after a contraction or after a part of a name used as a whole:

Ben Brown *isn't* here.

Note: Only one period is necessary at the end of a sentence even if it ends with an abbreviation, but a question mark (506) may follow a period used after an abbreviation at the end of a sentence:

A great battle was fought in the year 490 B.C.

What battle was fought in the year 490 B.C.?

467   Three periods are used to show omission in quoted material:

"He did his best . . . , yet he never quite succeeded."

A fourth period is used at the end of a sentence.

Note: The period is used between the integral and decimal parts of a mixed fraction and between figures indicating dollars and cents:

The lake is 62.35 miles long.

With the discount it cost $14.22.

Semicolon

468   Use a semicolon between two clauses of a compound sentence (401) when they are not joined by a conjunction (355-359) unless they are very short and are used informally (475):

The rain came in torrents; we did not know what to do. (This may be punctuated as two sentences.)

He came, he saw, he went away.

469   The semicolon is used between clauses of a compound sentence which are joined by conjunctive adverbs (311), such as *therefore, hence, however, nevertheless, accordingly, thus, then:*

The day was very cold; therefore we did not go for a ride.

470   The semicolon is often used between clauses which are joined by conjunctions if the clauses are long, or if the clauses have commas within themselves:

John arrived last night, I am told; but because his plane was late, he could not come to the party.

Note: The semicolon may be used for clearness:

> We invited Don Webb, the captain of the team; Sue Mills, the president of our class; and Joe Wynn, the chairman of our group.

471   The semicolon usually precedes *as, namely,* or *thus* when used to introduce examples:

> Four boys were mentioned; namely, Henry, Clarence, Merle, and Clyde.

Colon

472   The colon is used to introduce formally a word, a list, examples, a statement or question, a series of statements, or a long quotation. An expression such as *as follows* or *the following* usually precedes the list:

> He brought the following fruits: apples, peaches, pears.

473   A colon is used after the salutation of a business letter and is used between the parts of a number denoting time:

> Dear Sir: He came at 6:15 this morning.

Comma

474   A great many good authorities insist upon using a comma between the clauses of a compound sentence (401) if they are joined by such a conjunction as *but, for, or, and.* Other authorities contend that the use of the comma here is merely optional. If, however, the clauses are long and have commas within them, a semicolon should be used to separate them (see 470):

> Robert entered the race, but he did not win.
> Robert entered the race but he did not win. (also accepted)

475   Very short clauses making up a series and not joined by conjunctions may be separated by commas (468, 483):

> She came, she looked, she went away.

476   An adverbial clause (398) which precedes a main clause (386), unless it is very short, is set off by a comma:

> When my cousin came to spend the day with me, she found me at work.
> If you expect to succeed, you must prepare yourself.

The comma is usually omitted when the adverbial clause follows the main clause:

> My cousin found me at work when she came to spend the day with me.

477   A comma should be used to set off *yes* or *no* used as mild interjections or sentence adverbs:

> Yes, you may go.

Other mild interjections (44), such as *ah, oh, well, why,* are set off by commas when exclamation marks would be too strong:

> Ah, well, who can tell what may happen?

478 Nonrestrictive phrases and clauses should be set off from the rest of the sentence by a comma or commas. A nonrestrictive phrase or clause is a nonessential phrase or clause; that is, it is a phrase or a clause which could be omitted without changing the meaning of the main clause:

Edgar Allan Poe, who wrote "The Raven," is a great American poet. (The clause *who wrote "The Raven"* is not necessary to the meaning of the main clause.)

Boys who study will learn. (The clause *who study* is necessary to explain which boys will learn.)

The girl who sells the tickets is an honor student. (*Who sells the tickets* is necessary to explain which girl is an honor student.)

Jane Gray, who sells the concert tickets, is a member of our class. (The clause is not necessary; it merely explains that the girl sells tickets.)

The boy, seeing the cloud, hurried home. (The phrase is not necessary to explain *boy*.)

The girl holding the flag is Margaret. (The phrase is necessary to tell which girl is Margaret.)

Wishing to see the parade, we went to town early. (A participial phrase, 380-3, which stands at the beginning of a sentence is followed by a comma.)

The task being done, we went home. (absolute, 95)

479 Items of a parenthetical nature are set off by commas. Two commas are necessary when the expression is within the sentence and no other mark is used. These items include persons addressed, appositives, items in addresses and dates, as well as independent phrases and clauses:

Will you help me, Harry, with this work?

Nan Gray, my favorite cousin, is here.

Tom came from Dallas, Texas, yesterday.

Jane was born on June 12, 1952, in Wichita.

That boy is, I believe, a dependable chap.

Note: When an appositive (97) is a part of the proper name, or is closely connected with the word it explains, no comma is used:

Edward the Confessor was there.

My cousin Nell lives in Arizona.

480 A direct informal quotation equivalent to a sentence should be separated from explanatory matter by a comma or commas. But a sentence quoted within another sentence may be so closely connected with the rest of the sentence that no comma is needed:

The girl said, "Wait for me."

"Wait for me," the girl said.

"Wait," the girl said, "until I come."

Her cheerful greeting was always "How do you do today?"

Warning: Use no comma before an indirect quotation or a title in quotation marks unless there is a need:

Fred said that he went to Chicago.

Longfellow wrote "The Psalm of Life."

481 Items in a date are set off by commas:

They were married on Tuesday, May 6, 1946.

Note: In a date consisting of month and year only, the use of commas is optional:

In *August, 1965* (or *August 1965*) we were on vacation.

482 Use commas for explanatory matter in connection with a direct quotation, unless stronger punctuation is necessary (495):

"It is time," she said, "for me to go home."

"It is time to go," she said; "it is very late."

483 Use commas to separate the items of a series of words, phrases, or short clauses:

The farmer sold corn, hay, oats, potatoes, and wheat.

They came from east, from west, from north, and from south.

He arose, he smiled, he began to speak.

484 A series of adjectives of the same rank modifying the same noun are separated by commas unless they are joined by conjunctions. No comma is used after the last adjective:

We saw tall, slender, graceful trees.

A steep and narrow path led on.

Note: When the adjective next to the noun seems to be a part of the noun, no comma is used before it:

He is a courteous young man. (*Courteous* modifies *young man.*)

485 A comma may be used for clearness:

Ever since, Frank has been a better boy.

You would, would you?

Quotation Marks

486 Quotation marks are used to enclose a direct quotation. They are not used with indirect quotations:

"You are to blame," she said.

He said *that he would go home.*

487 Quotation marks or italics are used to distinguish words or letters referred to merely as words or letters. (Italics are preferred in this use.)

You may parse the word "they" in that sentence.

Note: Never use quotation marks where they are not required by the rules of mechanics. Do not use quotation marks for mere emphasis or adornment as in sign painting or on cafe menus.

488   Quotation marks are used with the titles of articles, of chapters of books, and of short poems and stories (italics are used for titles of books, periodicals, names of ships, etc., 514B):

He read Whittier's "Maud Muller."

I read Hawthorne's *The Scarlet Letter.*

Note: One line drawn under a word indicates that it should be italicized in print.

489   A long quotation may have quotation marks at the beginning of each paragraph and at the end of the last paragraph. However, most long quotations are set off by additional indention or by smaller type or by both, and in such case no quotation marks are used. (See examples in 518, 521-524B, 525C.)

490   In reporting conversation, each speech or fragment of speech (494), no matter how short, should be in quotation marks. An uninterrupted quotation in one paragraph, though long, should have but one set of quotation marks (beginning and ending):

"Do you know me?" he asked.

"I am not sure," she replied, "that I have ever met you."

"I am your old schoolmate, Edgar Jones," he explained.

491   Nicknames and words or phrases used ironically may be put in quotations:

My friend "Shorty" was there.

His "limousine" was a jalopy. (Be sparing of this use; it may become very annoying.)

Note: Usually quotations are omitted from nicknames after the first use or when the nickname (such as *Babe* Ruth) is well known. Many people also use quotation marks to distinguish technical terms and slang. Often it is better to avoid the use of slang and faulty diction than to apologize for it with quotation marks. If the slang phrase is too expressive to admit substitution, assume responsibility for using it instead of quoting it.

492   A quotation within a quotation should be enclosed in single quotation marks, and a quotation within that should be in double marks:

"I was surprised," Mary admitted, "when he said, 'I agree with Shakespeare, "All the world's a stage." ' "

493   A question mark or an exclamation mark is placed inside the quotation marks if it is a part of the quotation; outside, if it applies to the main clause. The period or the comma is always placed before the quotation marks (note example in 492); the semicolon is placed outside:

"Are you ill?" she asked.

Did Father say, "Wait until tororrow"?

Tom said, "Don't wait for me"; then he turned and walked away.

"The music was beautiful," she remarked.

Note: If both the main clause of the sentence and the quotation are interrogative, only one question mark (506) is used:

Did Fred ask, "Where have you been?"

494 When a quotation is interrupted, an extra set of marks must be used:

"Come," he said, "as soon as you have the time."

495 There is often an erroneous impression among students that all interruptions of quotations are marked by commas. Use the marks which should be used regardless of the quotation:

"You have delayed too long already," he said. "Success does not come to him who tarries."

"I am wrong!" she exclaimed; "there is no denying that."

Apostrophe

496 Use the apostrophe to indicate the omission of letters from words. It should be placed immediately above the point of omission:

The man *isn't* here.

497 The apostrophe may be used with *s* to denote plurals of letters, figures, signs, symbols, and words considered merely as words (85):

She used two *a's*, three *b's*, two *8's* (or *8s*), two *and's* (or *ands*).

498 The apostrophe is used in forming the possessive of nouns and indefinite pronouns. To form the possessive singular, add the apostrophe and *s* (115):

The *bird's* song is beautiful.

He is *everyone's* friend.

To form the possessive of a singular or plural noun that does not end in *s*, add the apostrophe and *s* (115, 117):

The *salesman's* samples included *men's* hats.

To form the possessive plural of a noun whose plural ends in *s*, add an apostrophe only (116):

Boys' suits are on sale.

Note: Some words admit of two forms (115):

Burns' or *Burns's, James'* or *James's*. (The second form seems preferred.)

Warning: The possessives of the personal pronouns such as *its, his, hers, ours, yours,* and *theirs* (141) do not use the apostrophe. But indefinite pronouns, such as *either, one,* and *other,* do use the apostrophe:

The cat wants *its* (not *it's*) dinner. (*Its* is **possessive.**)

It's time to go home. (*It's* is a **contraction,** 141, 496.)

One must do *one's* duty.

The apostrophe is often omitted from proper names in special cases (some geographic names, organization or company names, etc.):

Pikes Peak, Citizens National Bank, Teachers College.

Dash

499 A dash is used to mark a sudden change or break in a sentence:
The boy went—where did he go?
"There is no——" The speaker could not go on.(No period is needed after a dash which breaks off a sentence.)
Smith told me—but don't mention this—that he was bankrupt.

500 The dash may be used to set off a parenthetic group, especially when the parenthetic expression contains commas:
His food—nuts, berries, small game—was adequate for survival.

501 The dash may be used before a summarizing statement:
He planned, he worked, he sacrificed—all these he did that he might succeed.

502 The dash may be used for emphasis:
For a thousand dollars—a mere thousand dollars—he betrayed his friend.

Note: A double-length dash may be used to indicate the omission of words or letters:
Have you see Captain H—— lately?

Parentheses and Brackets

503 Parentheses may be used to enclose matter apart from the main thought:
If you come to see me (and I hope you do come), be sure to bring your camera.

Matter enclosed in parentheses within a sentence, even though it forms a complete declarative or imperative sentence, need not begin with a capital and need not end with a period. But if it is interrogative or exclamatory, it ends with the appropriate mark (506, 507):
She says that you insulted her (did you?) and that she hasn't forgiven you.

504 A punctuation mark belonging to matter given before that set off by parentheses should be placed after the second parenthesis mark (see the first example sentence given in 503):
When you receive your appointment (and I hope you receive it soon), you must tell me of your plans.

If a separate sentence is placed in parentheses, the final punctuation is placed inside the parentheses:
(These theories will be further explained in the next chapter.)

505 Brackets are used to enclose explanatory matter which one inserts in quoting another writer:
It was this poem ["The Raven"] that made Poe famous.

Question Mark

506 Place a question mark after every direct question. Although the very short declarative sentence (25) within parentheses (465) does not require a period, the short interrogative sentence (27) thus used must close with a question mark (503):

Have you seen my new hat?

When you come to see me (why not come soon?), I will tell you of my trip to Denver.

Note: If the main clause of a sentence and the dependent clause are both interrogative (27), only one question mark (493) is used. No question mark is used after an indirect question. After a polite request a period should be used instead of a question mark:

Did the coach inquire, "When did you return?"

He asked what the trouble was.

Will you please send the check at once.

507 A question mark within parentheses expresses uncertainty about dates or other information:

Lucretius, 96(?)-55 B.C.

In sentences it is usually better to use *about* or *probably* than the question mark.

Exclamation Mark

508 The exclamation mark is used after words, expressions, or sentences to show strong feeling or forceful utterance:

Fire! Fire!   How terrible it was!

An exclamation within parentheses retains the exclamation mark (503):

She left the door unlocked (how thoughtless!) and drove to the store.

Hyphen

509 A hyphen should be used to join words combined into a single adjective modifier: *well-to-do, self-supporting, far-flung.*

Adverbs ending in *ly* are not usually changed into compound modifiers: a *beautifully illustrated* story.

510 The hyphen is omitted when certain compound modifiers follow the word modified, but other compounds retain the hyphen in this position:

His mother is *self-supporting.*   His mother is *well liked.*

Use your dictionary as a guide to correct handling of compounds.

511 Hyphens should be used in compound numbers from twenty-one to ninety-nine.

512 Fractions are hyphenated only when used as modifiers:
One half of the book is finished. (noun)
The box is two-thirds full. (adverb)
He won by a two-thirds majority. (adjective)

513 New compounds are hyphenated, but after a time the hyphen may be omitted and the compound written as a solid. Words which have but recently lost the hyphen are *tonight, tomorrow, today.* A good dictionary is the only safe guide to the correct use of hyphens.

514 When it is necessary to divide a word at the end of a line, the division should be made between syllables, and a hyphen should be placed at the end of the line. Never place a hyphen at the beginning of a line.

ABBREVIATIONS and CONTRACTIONS

514A The following rules should be observed in using abbreviations and contractions (see also 466):

1. The use of many abbreviations in formal writing indicates carelessness on the part of the writer. However, there are a few abbreviations which are used regularly in formal writing: *A.B., B.C., a.m., p.m.* (when used with figures), *Mr., Mrs., Dr.* (when used with names).

2. It is considered impolite to abbreviate titles such as the following when used before the last name only: *captain, general, colonel, professor, president.*

3. The old rule was to place a period after each abbreviation, but there are a growing number of exceptions to the rule (see 466).

Contractions and Roman numerals used in sentences do not require periods after them:

He *doesn't* live here.   James *II* was king of England.

Periods are not used with scientific or technical symbols: H_2SO_4, sin, tan, cos.

ITALICS (Underlining)

514B The following rules should be observed in using italics:

1. In writing longhand and in typing, place one line under a word to indicate that it should be printed in italics.

2. Italicize foreign terms which have not become naturalized. The dictionary is the only safe guide in determining these.

3. Italicize a word, phrase, or letter used as a subject of discussion (see also 487):   The word *receive* is often misspelled.

4. Use italics to indicate the titles of books, magazines, newspapers, paintings, and the names of ships, aircraft, and man-made satellites:

We have just read *Lord of the Flies* by William Golding.

On February 20, 1962, John H. Glenn, Jr., made three orbits of the earth in *Friendship 7*.

5. Most authorities agree that an article (276) or the name of a city used in the title of a magazine or newspaper need not be italicized:

We read the Kansas City *Star*.

6. It is permissible to italicize a word for emphasis, but this use of italics should be rare:

He *would* go back in spite of everything.

NUMERALS

514C   The following rules should be observed in writing numerals:

1. Dates, street numbers, page numbers, decimals, and percents should be written in figures:

Columbus discovered America on *October 12, 1492*.
He lives at *16* Spruce Street.
Jim got *60* percent of the vote for class president.

2. The sign $ is not used for a sum less than one dollar:

The knife cost *sixty-five cents*.

3. The general rule for writing numbers is to spell out the number if it may be done in one or two words; otherwise, it should be written in figures:

He gave me a *thousand* dollars.
He gave me *1397* copies of the paper.

4. When several numbers are mentioned in a short space, use figures for all.

5. A number which represents a person's age or one denoting the hour of the day is usually spelled out:

At *three* o'clock there is to be a meeting of the boys who are between *sixteen* and *eighteen* years of age.

6. Do not begin a sentence with figures:

Six hundred twenty-five (not 625) students were at the meeting.

7. It is not necessary, except in special instances, to place numerals in parentheses after writing numbers; but when they are used, each should follow the number it repeats:

I am sending you *fifteen (15)* bushels of wheat.

8. In technical, mathematical, and business writing figures are generally used:

125 square feet, *$6.00* per pound, *4½* percent, *9.6* meters.

Five: *THE PARAGRAPH*

STRUCTURE AND ANALYSIS

515 What Is a Paragraph? The paragraph is usually thought of as a group of sentences developing a single topic, but a paragraph may consist of a single sentence. Sometimes several paragraphs may be needed to develop a topic.

516 Length of the Paragraph. The length of the paragraph in general writing is determined primarily by the extent to which the topic is discussed. This rule, however, is not so arbitrary that it may not be modified, as for instance in the business letter (536),* in which the short paragraph is more effective than the longer one. In dialogue, of course, each speech is separately paragraphed as a rule.

517 Paragraph Sense. Everyone should develop a paragraph sense, just as one develops a sentence sense (34). This sense may be developed by thinking in topics and by adhering strictly to each topic under discussion.

518 Topic Sentence. The sentence which presents the topic to be discussed is called the **topic sentence.** It is often placed at the beginning of the paragraph, but it can occur at any point, and its position should be varied to avoid monotony. The paragraph following, from Emerson's "Compensation," illustrates the beginning topic sentence:

> *A man cannot speak but he judges himself.* With his will or against his will he draws his portrait to the eye of his companions by every word. Every opinion reacts on him who utters it. It is a threadball thrown at a mark, but the other end remains in the thrower's bag. Or rather, it is a harpoon thrown at the whale, unwinding, as it flies, a coil of cord in the boat, and, if the harpoon is not good, or not well thrown, it will go nigh to cut the steersman in twain or to sink the boat.

Note: Often no one sentence expresses the topic. But make sure that, except for transition paragraphs, a topic can be expressed for each paragraph.

518A Developing the Topic. There are many ways of developing the topic, some of the most common being the use of **details, examples, comparison** or **contrast, cause and effect,** or a combination of any two or more of these methods. Usually two or more of these methods are used in the development of a paragraph. Although the name of each method indicates its nature, an illustration is given for each of the first three:

1. **Details.** Giving details makes a topic more vivid and develops at

---

* *Numbers in parentheses refer to sections of this book.*

more length what is suggested in the topic. Here is a familiar paragraph from *The Legend of Sleepy Hollow* which is a good example:

> All was now bustle and hubbub in the late quiet schoolroom. The
> scholars were hurried through their lessons, without stopping at trifles;
> those who were nimble skipped over half with impunity, and those
> who were tardy, had a smart application now and then in the rear, to
> quicken their speed, or help them over a tall word. Books were flung
> aside without being put away on the shelves, inkstands were over-
> turned, benches thrown down, and the whole school was turned loose
> an hour before the usual time, bursting forth like a legion of young
> imps, yelping and racketing about the green, in joy at their early
> emancipation.

2. **Examples.** Concrete examples are given to illustrate the general
suggestion of the topic:

> Riverside Park is noted for the beauty and variety of its native trees.
> Along the river to the south are many excellent specimens of elm,
> sycamore, cottonwood, and hackberry. To the west, covering several
> acres, is a grove of tall, beautiful black walnut trees, shading here
> and there a less stately mulberry. To the north the park abounds
> in large shapely oaks, some of which thrust out protecting arms above
> clumps of timid redbuds. Other less prominent specimens scattered
> throughout the park are ash, box elder, and Osage orange.

3. **Contrast.** Through contrast, differences are made to stand out
more prominently. Notice the effect of this method in the paragraph
below, from Irving's "The Country Church":

> As I have brought these families into contrast, I must notice their
> behavior in church. That of the nobleman's family was quiet, serious,
> and attentive. Not that they appeared to have any fervor of devo-
> tion, but rather a respect for sacred things, and sacred places, in-
> separable from good breeding. The others, on the contrary, were
> in a perpetual flutter and whisper; they betrayed a continual con-
> sciousness of finery, and the sorry ambition of being the wonders of
> a rural congregation.

When the development of a topic is the explanation of some process,
such as building something, it is best to follow the natural order of
the procedure. That is, the procedure in developing a topic sug-
gesting the construction of an article would be from the selection of
the materials on through the different stages in the natural order of
construction.

519   Mechanics of Writing Paragraphs.

1. Indent the first line of each paragraph. In writing longhand, it
is customary to indent about an inch; in typing, the usual indentation
is five or ten spaces.

Note: Some business firms of high standing do not indent typewritten paragraphs in their letters. Sometimes, too, printers begin paragraphs at the margin.

2. Do not leave a part of a line blank except at the close of the paragraph.

3. Except when the length of the paragraph is arbitrary, as it is in dialogue, it should seldom be made either extremely short or long.

4. In dialogue, begin a paragraph with each change of speaker.

5. Keep the left margin of the paragraph straight and the right margin reasonably straight. Indentations should be uniform.

6. Make the transition from paragraph to paragraph easy and natural, sometimes by the use of appropriate transition words (522), but always by proper arrangement.

Paragraph Requirements

520 The paragraph, like the sentence (419-421), must have **unity, coherence,** and **emphasis.**

521 **Unity of the paragraph** is attained when every sentence bears directly upon the topic of that particular paragraph. Any departure from the central topic means that a new paragraph should be formed. In the following paragraph the italicized sentence is irrelevant and therefore should be eliminated:

You will find in this car all the qualities you desire most in a motor car—economy, style, comfort, efficiency, endurance. With its low first cost and inexpensive operation it has long been the acknowledged economy leader. It is also a style leader, and it offers every modern comfort expected in even the most expensive type of car. *Owners are enthusiastic about it because of its easy steering.* In speed and safety and sureness of high performance it defines competition. Year after year it continues to give superior service unhampered by the inconvenience and expense of repair.

522 **Coherence in the paragraph** results from the correct arrangement of the parts of a paragraph—an arrangement in which each part of the paragraph leads to the next. This linking of the parts of the paragraph is often aided by the use of appropriate transitional words, but too many such words results in a heavy, stilted style. Careful arrangement is the important means of attaining coherence. Transition words are so numerous that one may be found to suit the exact need of almost any transition. Some of the more commonly used of these words are *furthermore, however, for this reason, consequently, in addition, notwithstanding, all things considered, to this end, hence, above all, for example, as a consequence, on the contrary nevertheless, as a result, but, otherwise, yet, still, meanwhile, presently, finally, in conclusion, for instance, therefore,* and *accordingly.* The paragraph below, although somewhat artificial, illustrates the smooth use of transition words. But to see the importance of arrangement, try placing the next to the last sentence as the concluding sentence. This will show the loss in force of the paragraph which is not coherent:

> You may be sure that I am pleased with the adjustment you have made about the returned goods. This adjustment is in keeping with the fine spirit of honesty and fairness which you have continually shown me in the years in which I have been doing business with you. As a consequence of your excellent treatment, I have continued to favor you with the bulk of my orders. In addition, I have used my influence to turn other business to you. As in the past, I shall continue to give you evidence of my appreciation in this practical way.

523 **Emphasis in the paragraph** results from giving stress to the important ideas. If more space is given to the important ideas than to the unimportant, there is possibility of interfering with unity and coherence; therefore it may be best to give emphasis by position. The beginning or the close of the paragraph is the most emphatic position. The paragraph below from "The Mask of the Red Death" by Poe is a good illustration of proper emphasis in the paragraph. Note how by position the emphasis is given by *Red Death*. It is obvious that a shifting of the last sentence to the middle of the paragraph would weaken the entire effect:

> And now was acknowledged the presence of the Red Death. He had come like a thief in the night. And one by one dropped the revelers in the blood-bedewed halls of their revel, and each died in the despairing posture of his fall. And the life of the ebony clock went out with that of the last of the gay. And the flames of the tripods expired. And Darkness and Decay and the Red Death held illimitable dominion over all.

FORMS OF DISCOURSE

524 There are four types of expression known as **forms of discourse**, and every paragraph illustrates one of these types or a combination of two or more of them. These four forms are **exposition, description, narration, argumentation**.

Exposition

524A **Exposition** is explaining, and it is the form most frequently used. It is, however, often closely associated with the other forms, particularly with description. In fact, exposition and description are so closely blended sometimes that it is difficult to distinguish between them. Exposition depends for its effectiveness on the use of accurate, concrete words instead of vague, abstract terms. The paragraph below, from *Living Today—6* (by Cole, Cole, and Appleyard, © 1958 by McCormick-Mathers Publishing Company, Inc.) illustrates clear exposition in very simple, accurate terms:

When you speak, your vocal chords vibrate. The vibrations cause changes in the pressure of the air. Waves of sound are set up. When the sound waves reach another person, they strike the eardrum. The eardrum vibrates according to the changing pressure of the air on it. The person hears.

Description

524B Description is picturing in words. As has been pointed out (524A), it is closely associated with the other forms, particularly exposition, with which it is often almost inseparably blended. Pure description is seldom met with in discourse, for it needs the other forms to give it movement. It is made vivid by the use of meaningful words, particularly adjectives (266) and nouns (37). The paragraph given below, from Irving's *Rural Life in England,* is a good illustration of description. Note the descriptive words *imposing, vast, vivid, gigantic, rich, solemn, woodland, silent, natural, glassy, sequestered, quivering, yellow, sleeping, limpid, rustic, sylvan, green, dank, classic:*

> Nothing can be more imposing than the magnificence of English park scenery. Vast lawns that extend like sheets of vivid green, with here and there clumps of gigantic trees, heaping up rich piles of foilage; the solemn pomp of groves and woodland glades, with the deer trooping in silent herds across them; the hare bounding away to the covert; or the pheasant, suddenly bursting upon the wing; the brook taught to wind in natural meanderings or expand into a glassy lake the sequestered pool, reflecting the quivering trees, with the yellow leaf sleeping on its bosom, and the trout roaming fearlessly about its limpid waters; while some rustic temple of sylvan statue, grown green and dank with age, gives an air of classic sanctity to the seclusion.

Narration

524C Narration is a rehearsal of events which may have been either real or imaginary; it is the telling of a story, whether the story is truth or fiction. It is usually associated with exposition and description, and it must give the effect of movement from event to event. The many stories with which we are familiar are examples of narration. Those who write or tell stories should observe these precautions:

Make a prompt, effective beginning; stick to the story; tell the story simply; end it promptly.

Argumentation

524D Argumentation is an effort to show by logical arrangement of facts that a statement is true or false, as in a mathematical demonstration such as proof of a proposition in geometry. When one attempts to change another to a new conviction in a matter, one explains facts favorable to that conviction: this is **argumentation.** To be successful in argumentation, one must exercise the same tact and skills as in the other forms. Much toward the general good may be achieved through argumentation, but we gain little through its use in the ordinary contacts of everyday life (550A).

DEVELOPMENT OF CREATIVE EXPRESSION

524E **Creative expression** is the communication of a feeling or experience that is worth sharing with others just for its own sake. This is the type of expression which at its best gives us our literature. But all of us, whether we have the urge or the genius to become great creative artists, should give thought to creative expression, for it will help us to observe more closely the things about us. We become more critical of ourselves and others and thus more able to analyze our own behavior and more sympathetic with the behavior of others. Through this type of expression we may eventually have a broader understanding of life and its problems.

Précis Writing

525 **Ability to Condense Expression.** It is important that one should develop the ability to express his thoughts in well-organized paragraphs of the different forms of discourse (524), and it is of no less importance that one should learn to condense his meaning into the fewest possible words. One should also acquire the ability to condense the expression of others to the fewest words consistent with clearness. Such a condensed form of expression retains the thought of the original and gives emphasis to it. This form is called **précis.**

525A **Précis.** A standard definition of précis is a "brief summary of essential points, statements, or facts." It differs from a paraphrase in that it is much shorter and more precisely and accurately written. It must retain in a few words the ideas of the original, and these ideas must be clearly and forcefully expressed. The length of the précis may vary with the intensity of the thought, but a good general average would be to reduce the number of words to one third or one fourth the original. The writer of the précis must understand all the meaning of the expression to be condensed (525E).

525B **Suggestions for Précis Writing.** Précis writing is excellent exercise for inexperienced writers who have a tendency to wordiness (444A). Here are some general suggestions:

1. Be sure you understand what you are trying to condense.

2. Follow the original without changing the order of the thought.

3. Use your own words.

4. Write as clearly and forcefully as possible.

525C **Illustration.** Below is an illustration of précis writing in which each of five summaries of a paragraph is rated by expert authority.

The original paragraph is given first, followed by the instructions for grading the summaries. Following the instructions, are five summaries, and in parentheses to the left of each is marked the ranking given it by the author of the test from which this extract is taken. (The extract is "Selection V, Form A," from the *Poley Précis Test,* a standard test by Irvin C. Poley, published by Public School Publishing Company, Bloomington, Illinois. The extract is used with the permission of the publishers.)

> Vandalism in the parks is all too typical of one side of the American character. We seem incapable of bearing in mind an idea of decency in the abstract. As guests, if our host is a friend, we treat him with courtesy; but if he is unknown and not at hand to watch us we concede him no rights whatever; as hunters borrowing somebody's land we drop cigarettes and start forest fires; as campers borrowing somebody's woods we have a litter of cans and refuse that is notorious. . . . We are callous to the idea that things ought not to be destroyed, no matter who owns them or who will use them. . . . Park vandals are guests of the public, and they should have enough regard for the host not to destroy his property. They use the parks in common with many other people and they should have a thought to the comfort of others.
>
> Editorial, New York *World.*

Following this are five summaries of the paragraph just given. In the parentheses to the left of the précis which you think best expresses the thought of the original paragraph, write *R.* The other four summaries may be wrong (not accurate) or inadequate. Put *X* in the parentheses to the left of each summary (paragraph) that is wrong; that is, when there is an actual error of statement. Put *I* in the parentheses to the left of each summary that is merely inadequate; that is, when, although there is no error of statement, the central thought of the original paragraph has been missed.

(R) a. Americans are apt to be discourteous in their treatment of public parks. They should remember that consideration is due as much to an absent or public host as to a present or private one.

(X) b. In America the parks are littered with trash, especially cigarettes, which may start a forest fire. Private property should be respected as much as public.

(X) c. Private property should be respected as much as public property, if not more. Parks are sure to be littered with refuse, and public camping sites are spoiled.

(I) d. If hunters borrow land, they should be careful not to drop cigarettes and thus start a fire. Campers should not leave a litter of refuse behind them; even if they do not know the owner, they should be considerate of his property.

(X) e. Americans should learn to get along pleasantly with people they meet in the park. The public is our host, and individuals should try to act as courteously to another as they do in Europe.

Critical Reading

525D   Reading. Reading is usually done for one of two reasons—to get the thought, or to get the mechanical construction of the expression, the spelling, the grammar, the punctuation and capitalization. The latter type is usually referred to as **proofreading.** The two types are discussed separately here.

525E   Reading for Thought. One who reads to get the thought may do so for any one of several reasons. One may read the newspapers through mere curiosity or read magazines or books from a desire to know the opinions of others. A more serious purpose of the reader may be to gather material for a paper or a speech through extensive reading in a library. The latter type of reading is usually accompanied with note-taking, the purpose of which is to gather facts.

Every pupil should learn to grasp quickly the main ideas as he reads. He may get the principal facts in a newspaper article by reading the headlines and leads. He should train himself to glean from every paragraph the facts necessary in writing brief, clear notes or a précis (525A). Accurate reading and expert précis writing go hand in hand, both being invaluable aids to one who wishes to master effective expression.

525F   Proofreading. In addition to learning to get the thought from written expression, one must learn to detect mechanical errors in it. Reading for the purpose of correcting mechanical errors is called **proofreading,** though in the strictest sense this term is applied only to the correcting of proof sheets for printing. You may use any simple system of marking errors in proofreading your own work or the work of others. Complete rules for correcting such errors are conveniently arranged in this book. Those interested in reading real proof will find a list of standard symbols in *Webster's Seventh New Collegiate Dictionary,* pages 1051-1053.

Writing Verse

526.   Expression in Verse. Verse is a form of composition which is very different from prose. It is so constructed that it has rhythm, and this rhythm is generally produced by a regular arrangement of stressed and unstressed syllables.

Writing verse is good practice for one who wishes to acquire skill in the use of words that are not only expressive but also pleasant in sound. In addition, the writing of light or humorous verse may be made very enjoyable. It gives variety to expression, which, in prose, has a tendency to become monotonous. The next few paragraphs explain the structure of verse.

526A   Verse Forms. Before one attempts to write verse, one should become familiar with the simple mechanics of versification given here.

Verse. The term *verse* may be applied to rhythmical composition in general, but in a more restricted sense it may indicate a line of verse. A verse, then, of poetry is one line, not a group of lines.

Stanza. A stanza is a group of lines (verses) usually bound together by some rhyme scheme (526H).

Foot. A foot is simply a unit of measurement of rhythm in verse, consisting usually of one accented syllable and one or more unaccented syllables.

Kinds of Feet. There are four kinds of feet in popular use, though there are others less used. The four are **iambic, trochaic, anapaestic,** and **dactyllic.**

1. Iambic. The iambic foot consists of one unaccented syllable followed by one accented: *ex-pél.*

2. Trochaic. A trochaic foot is made up of one accented syllable followed by one unaccented: *beáu-ty.*

3. Anapaestic. An anapaestic foot has two unaccented syllables followed by one accented: *in-ter-véne.*

4. Dactylic. A dactylic foot has one accented syllable followed by two unaccented: *beáu-ti-ful.*

526B   Number of Feet in a Line. A line (verse) is classified by the number of feet it contains. A line of one foot is a **monometer;** two feet, **dimeter;** three feet, **trimeter;** four feet, **tetrameter;** five feet, **pentameter;** six feet, **hexameter;** seven feet, **heptameter;** and eight feet, **octameter.**

526C   Name of Line. A line gets its name from the number and kind of feet it contains. For example, a line of five iambic feet is called **iambic pentameter.** Here are illustrations taken from familiar poems:

(iambic tetrameter)   I think | that I | shall nev- | er see. ("Trees")

(trochaic tetrameter)   Tell me | not in | mourn-ful | num-bers. ("Psalm of Life")

(anapaestic tetrameter)   For the moon | nev-er beams | with-out bring- | ing me dreams. ("Anabel Lee")

(dactylic hexameter)   Black were her | eyes as the | ber-ry that | grows on the | thorn by the | way-side. ("Evangeline")

526D   Rhyme. Rhyme is correspondence, in two or more words, of ending sounds beginning with the last accented vowel. The preceding consonant sounds should be different, but rhymes are not always perfect:

Rhymes: *relate, sedate; willing, fulfilling*
Imperfect Rhymes: *relate, elate; imply, reply*

526E   Rhythm. Rhythm is the more or less regular recurrence of accented and unaccented syllables. Rhythm is necessary to verse, but rhyme is not. Verse in regular rhythm without rhyme is called **blank verse.** Another kind of verse without rhyme is called **free verse.** It has rhythmical cadence, but does not depend on the strict arrangement of accented and unaccented syllables.

526F   Blank Verse. Any unrhymed verse may be called blank verse, but this term applies especially to iambic pentameter, the type used in Shakespeare's plays.

526G   Rhyme Scheme. A stanza usually has a regular rhyme scheme. That is, each stanza in a given poem has corresponding lines which rhyme with each other. Rhyme scheme is represented by letters of the alphabet; a first rhyme is represented by *a*, a second by *b*, and so on.

526H   Stanza Forms. Some of the stanza forms much used are the **sonnet** (526J-526L), the **limerick** (526N), and the **quatrain.** The example of the quatrain given below is from Longfellow's "A Psalm of Life." It is made up of four trochaic tetrameter lines (526C) rhyming alternately *(a, b, a, b):*

> Lives of great men all remind us
> We can make our lives sublime,
> And, departing, leave behind us
> Footprints on the sands of time.

526J   Sonnet. The sonnet is a form which has long been popular. It consists of fourteen iambic pentameter lines with a strict rhyme scheme. There are two well-known forms of the sonnet, the **Italian,** or **Petrarchan,** and the **English,** or **Shakespearean.**

526K   Italian Sonnet. The Italian sonnet has the more rigid rhyme scheme, which demands but two rhymes in the first eight lines (octave) and restricts the rhyming of the last six lines (sestet). The rhyme of the octave is *a b b a a b b a.* The sestet may vary in the rhyme scheme, though the last two lines should not rhyme together. One correct form might be *c c d e d e.*

As an example of the Italian sonnet, here is one of the best known —that by Keats in which he confused the historical character Cortez with Balboa:

ON FIRST LOOKING INTO CHAPMAN'S HOMER

Much have | I trav | eled in | the realms | of gold,	(a)
And many goodly states and kingdoms seen;	(b)
Round many western islands have I been	(b)
Which bards in fealty to Apollo hold.	(a)
Oft of one wide expanse had I been told	(a)
That deep-brow'd Homer ruled as his demesne;	(b)
Yet did I never breathe its pure serene	(b)
Till I heard Chapman speak out loud and bold:	(a)
Then felt I like some watcher of the skies	(c)

When a new planet swims into his ken;	(d)
Or like stout Cortez when with eagle eyes	(c)
He stared at the Pacific—and all his men	(d)
Looked at each other with a wild surmise—	(c)
Silent, upon a peak in Darien.	(d)

526L   English Sonnet. The English, or Shakespearean, sonnet is made up of three quatrains with alternate rhyme and a rhyming couplet. The rhyme scheme used by Shakespeare is *a b a b c d c d e f e f g g.* One of Shakespeare's sonnets is given here:

SONNET LXIV

When I	have seen	by Time's	fell hand	defaced	(a)
The rich proud cost of outworn buried age;	(b)
When sometime lofty towers I see down-razed	(a)
And brass eternal slave to mortal rage;	(b)
When I have seen the hungry ocean gain	(c)
Advantage on the kingdom of the shore,	(d)
And the firm soil win of the watery main,	(c)
Increasing store with loss and loss with store;	(d)
When I have seen such interchange of state,	(e)
Or state itself confounded in decay;	(f)
Ruin hath taught me thus to ruminate,	(e)
That Time will come and take my love away.	(f)
This thought is as a death, which cannot choose	(g)
But weep to have that which it fears to lose.	(g)

526M   Types of Verse. There are many types of verse ranging from nonsense rhymes to the most exalted poetry. Only the higher types of verse should be called **poetry.** The limerick given below is a good example of light verse; the two sonnets in the two preceding sections are classed as poetry.

526N   Light Verse. Light or humorous verse may be written on a variety of subjects or in imitation of familiar poems or songs. A bit of writing in imitation of another is called a **parody.** The example of light verse given below is in limerick form. The first, second, and fifth lines of the limerick are anapaestic trimeter (526B-526D), and they rhyme together. The third and fourth lines are anapaestic dimeter, rhyming together. Any line of a limerick may begin with either one or two unaccented syllables.

BOB IN THE LAKE .

Bob knew that with Ev he was jake—
But words may an Eden unmake:
His *KNOWED* and *HAD WROTE*
Got Evelyn's goat—
She told him to jump in the lake.

Six: THE WHOLE COMPOSITION

PLANNING THE COMPOSITION

527 The Composition As a Unit. It is necessary that not only the sentences and paragraphs each maintain unity, coherence, and emphasis but also that the composition as a whole maintain these three qualities. The composition must be a unit with its parts so arranged as to show clearly their relationship. In addition, the most important ideas must be in the positions which give them the greatest emphasis: the beginning and the close.

528 Organizing Material. A very simple plan for news stories may be made by answering the questions *Who? When? Where? What? Why?*

Who—Our club
When—Last Thursday
Where—Glenwood Park
What—A picnic
Why—To entertain our new members

But an excellent general plan for organizing material for a composition is to jot down all thoughts on the subject as they occur, with no attempt at orderly arrangement, and then later to assemble the ideas in related groups for a complete outline. The topics in such an outline should be arranged in their natural order, somewhat as they are arranged in the outline below:

MARKET GARDENING
1. Deciding what to plant
2. Selecting seed
3. Preparing the soil
4. Planting
5. Cultivating
6. Gathering the products
7. Preparing the products for market
8. Selling the products

529 Topic Outline. The topic outline is made up of headings which indicate the main ideas in the composition. The terms of the same rank should be parallel. For instance, the main headings in the outline below are all nouns—"Pleasure," "Health," "Citizenship":

TENNIS IS A GOOD GAME FOR STUDENTS
I. Pleasure
    A. Relaxation from study
    B. Joy of competition

Numbers in parentheses refer to sections of this book.

II. Health
   A. Stimulation of bodily functions
   B. Increase in mental alertness
III. Citizenship
   A. Development of cooperation
   B. Development of regard for others

530 Sentence Outline. The sentence outline has complete sentences:

TENNIS IS A GOOD GAME FOR STUDENTS

I. It provides pleasure.
   A. The change from study to play brings relief.
   B. The thrill of competition is stimulating.
II. It promotes health.
   A. The outdoor exercise is good for the body.
   B. The keen interest in the game keeps the brain alert.
III. It develops good citizenship.
   A. The contact with others discourages selfishness.
   B. The rules of the game make necessary the regard for the rights of others.

Note: The **paragraph outline** is made up of complete paragraphs and is not so frequently used as the two forms given—the topic and the sentence.

WRITTEN COMPOSITION

531 There are two general classes of composition—**oral** and **written.** Writen composition will be discussed first.

532 Written composition includes every form of writing. This brief outline may give some idea of its great variety and importance.

533 Types of Written Composition. Of the many types of written composition the following are some of the most familiar: **fiction, biographies, essays, poetry, newspaper reporting,** and **letters.** Because the letter is the type of composition most widely used by people in general, it is discussed in detail.

534 Letters. Comparatively few people become professional writers, but everyone has occasion to write letters. The successful businessman must write letters of professional quality, and everyone must sometimes write letters of importance.

535 Classes of Letters. There are only two general classes of letters— **business** and **social.** The business letter includes all forms written for business purposes. The social letter varies from the informal letter of friendship to the most formal note. A letter, of course, may be a combination of the two classes.

Business Correspondence

536 Business Letters. The writing of business letters is not confined to those who are in business. Practically every person has occasion to write about transactions not included in the social affairs of life.

536A Importance of the Business Letter. A great part of the world's business is transacted through the exchange of letters; therefore the business letter is of tremendous importance. The very difficult art of business letter writing is challenging the finest talent in the world of commerce today.

536B Requirements of the Business Letter. Requirements of a good business letter are the following: **promptness, accuracy, clearness, economy, completeness, correctness, courtesy, neatness, friendliness, effective sentence construction, proper paragraphing, appropriate words properly spelled, and freedom from hackneyed expressions.** Each of these is worthy of short comment:

1. **Promptness.** A business letter should be answered at once.

2. **Accuracy.** A letter that is not accurate implies that the writer is either careless or lacking in ability.

3. **Clearness.** One of the first essentials of a business letter is clearness. Weak sentences (422-433) may cause confusion of meaning.

4. **Economy.** A letter should be so written that every word serves a distinct purpose. It should be as brief as is consistent with clearness and courtesy, but all sentences should be complete.

5. **Correctness.** No letter can otherwise be strong enough to overcome the handicap of incorrect language or form.

6. **Completeness.** A business letter should be so complete in itself as to make unnecessary any further correspondence to supplement it.

7. **Courtesy.** A business letter lacking in courtesy reflects discredit on the writer and on the business he represents. An effective means of showing courtesy is by stressing *you* rather than *I*.

8. **Neatness.** Neatness depends on the paper, margins, spacing, and typing. The paper is usually 8½ by 11 inches and of a good quality of white with envelopes to match. (Business letters should never be writen on stationery meant for social letters.) Margins should be so spaced that they are in correct proportion to the letter, and the typed space should appear as a picture correctly set in a frame. Usually single spacing is used except between paragraphs and parts of the letter, where spacing is double. The typing should be clear and free from erasures.

9. **Friendliness.** The best business letters are those which have a friendly tone.

10. **Effective Sentence Construction.** Make all sentences effective (419-421). See that they are free from weaknesses (422-433) and that they are varied (407-417).

11. **Proper Paragraphing.** The correct paragraphing of a business letter aids much in making its meaning clear. Long paragraphs are not so clear as shorter ones. Most writers of business letters prefer paragraphs of not more than six or eight lines. Proper arrangement of paragraphs is also vital.

12. **Proper Words.** Each word should be chosen to convey an exact meaning, and no word should ever be misspelled.

13. **Freedom from Hackneyed Expressions.** There are expressions in business correspondence which have become obsolete through overuse. No modern streamlined letter should be marred by even one of these relics. The following are a few of those that were once most frequently used: *and oblige, as per, at hand, beg to state, early date, enclosed herewith, esteemed favor, has come to hand, in the near future, kind favor, please note, recent date, we thank you kindly, we would advise, your favor, yours to hand.*

536C Parts of the Business Letter. There are six main parts to a business letter: **heading, inside address, salutation, body, complimentary close, signature.** Other parts of the business leter which might be included are the initials placed at the left lower margin of the dictated letter to indicate the dictator and the stenographer, and the outside address (on the envelope). These parts require separate discussion.

537 Heading of the Business Letter. The heading is placed at the upper right-hand corner (of paper that does not have a printed letterhead) and consists of the exact address of the writer and the date. The length may determine somewhat the number of lines it occupies, though it usually consists of three or four lines. The first line should give the smallest division, such as box number, name of building, or street and number; then comes the name of the city and the state, followed by the Zip Code number. The last line is the date.

The name of a city should not be abbreviated, and street numbers are written in figures. Most careful writers do not abbreviate the names of months in headings. Of course, where printed stationery is used, the letterhead gives all the heading except the date. The day of the month and the year are usually written in figures.

537A Form of the Heading. The heading may be either the **block type** or the **indented.** In the block type each line begins exactly the same distance from the right and left margins; in the indented type each succeeding line is spaced uniformly to the right. Illustrations are given below. The block form is almost always used in typing; the indented form may be used in writing longhand:

```
1255 Walnut Street          1255 Walnut Street
Denver, Colorado  80202      Denver, Colorado  80202
December 15, 19--             December 15, 19--
```

537B Punctuation of the Heading. Almost no punctuation appears in the heading except for the comma between the names of the city and state and the comma between the numbers indicating the day and year in the date.

538 Inside Address. The inside address should be placed at the left margin below the heading; and it should give the proper title, correct name, and complete address of the person for whom the letter is intended. The form should be the same as that of the heading.

```
Mr. Hugh J. Dunn
4230 Main Street
Houston, Texas  77002
```

539 Salutation. The salutation is placed at the left margin two spaces below the inside address. The following are appropriate salutations in greeting an individual: *Dear Mr. Hill, Dear Sir.* In letters addressed to a firm, *Gentlemen* is the most common greeting. *Dear Madam* is correct in addressing either a married or an unmarried woman, though *Dear Miss Hudson* is more frequently used in addressing an unmarried woman. The most formal salutation in addressing a man is *Sir,* and it is appropriate only in a letter to one of high rank.

Note: There are special forms of address and salutation for high dignitaries of church and state which should be followed exactly. *Webster's Seventh New Collegiate Dictionary,* under "Forms of Address," pages 1173-1176, gives a list of such forms.

540 Capitalization of the Salutation. If the salutation consists of but two words, both are capitalized; but in a salutation such as *My dear General Smith,* the *dear* is not capitalized.

541 Punctuation of the Salutation. The punctuation mark used after the salutation in a business letter is the colon (473). There is a tendency at present to add friendliness to the business letter; therefore the comma, which is less formal than the colon, might be used after the salutation of the more informal business letter to a friend.

542   Body. The body of the letter is the message. It should conform to all good rules of writing (see 536). The sentences should be made effective (see 407-444). The paragraphs should be short and forceful (see 520-523). All words should be well chosen, and each should add something to the effectiveness of the letter. Be careful to avoid worn-out expressions (see 536B) which brand a letter as stilted. Make your letter a part of you—give it personality.

The opening sentence is especially vital, for on its effectiveness may depend the fate of the entire message. The first sentence should be specific and it should make some personal appeal to the reader. It should stress *you*, not *I*. It should never begin with any of the following meaningless references to the receipt of a letter: *Pursuant to your request of the fifth, Answering your letter of October 5, We beg to acknowledge receipt of your letter of June 4, We are in receipt of your letter of May 9, Your letter of recent date at hand, Acknowledging yours of recent date, Supplementing your letter of March 16, We have your letter of April 3, Replying to yours of August 12, Complying with your request of recent date, Referring to your favor of June 6.* Such expressions were once popular, but they have gone to the scrap heap.

The closing sentence is also very important. It should leave the reader feeling that he has just made contact with a cordial, friendly human being.

If a letter is more than a page in length, the name of the person addressed the page number, and the date should be placed at the top of each additional page. The margin should be the same width. Not fewer than five lines should appear on the last page.

543   Complimentary Close. The complimentary close should be consistent with the other parts of the letter. It should never be preceded by the participial expressions once so popular, such as *Thanking you for your favor, Hoping this will be satisfactory, Awaiting your reply.* The last sentence should be complete, and it should say something vital. The close needs no such worn-out expressions as *I am* or *I remain* as an introduction. End the message with a forceful, appropriate sentence; then begin the close about the center of the page below. The following are correct in business letters: *Yours very truly, Yours sincerely, Sincerely yours.* The first word only of the close is capitalized, and the only punctuation mark used after it is the comma.

544   Signature. The signature is placed just below the close. Place the signature so that the first letter is exactly below the first letter of the close. Usually the writer's name is also typed just beneath the long-hand signature. Every letter should, of course, be signed in ink. The signature of a letter sent out by a business organization may include the name and position of the writer. The following is an example:

Frank G. Wilson

Frank G. Wilson, Sales Manager

In signing a letter, a married woman or a widow uses her own name, such as *Ann Clarke Brown,* not her married name, *Mrs. Frank R. Brown.* She may write *Mrs.* in parentheses before the name or she may write her married name in parentheses below the signature:

(Mrs.) *Louise C. Randall*   *Louise C. Randall*
                                       (Mrs. Robert J. Randall)

A divorcee has a choice in the use of her maiden name either with or without *Mrs.:*

(Miss) *Janice A. Jordan*
(Mrs.) *Janice A. Jordan*

In a dictated letter initials are typed at the lower left margin to identify the dictator and the stenographer. If there is an enclosure, it is indicated just under the initials:

FBJ:RHM	FBJ/rhm	FBJ-RHM
Encl.	Encl.	Enc.

544A Folding the Letter. The business letter is generally written on one side of a sheet of paper of commercial size, 8½ by 11 inches. When this is to be enclosed in an envelope of the larger size (usually No. 10—4⅛ by 9½ inches), fold up from the bottom about one third and down from the top slightly less. Place this in the envelope with the free edge at the top and toward the gummed flap (away from you). If the envelope to be used is of the smaller size (usually No. 6¾—3⅝ by 6½ inches), fold the lower part of the sheet over the upper so that the horizontal crease is slightly below the center; then fold the right-hand part so that the vertical crease is about one third from the right; then fold from the left so that the second vertical crease is slightly less than one third the width of the sheet from the left. Place this in the envelope with the free edge at the top and away from the gummed flap of the envelope (toward you). Be sure that all folds are straight and that all edges are even. The good effect of a letter may be lessened by careless or slovenly folding.

545 Outside Address. The outside address, or address on the envelope, should be the same in content as the inside address. The first line gives the name and the title of the person addressed, the second line gives the street number, and the third line gives the name of the city, the state, and the Zip Code number. The first line should be about the center of the envelope from top to bottom, though some writers prefer that it be slightly below. The name should be correctly spelled (a misspelled name is unforgivable), and it should be written exactly as the one addressed uses it. If a business title is long, it should be placed on a separate line. Abbreviations other than standard ones such as *Mr.* and *Mrs.*, and abbreviations such as *N.W.* for sections of a city, are not in favor with careful writers; therefore it is better to write out such words as the names of states, streets, and avenues. An address is usually single-spaced. Special directions, such as *General Delivery* and *Personal*, are placed in the lower left corner. The writer's name and address should be in the upper left corner. The following illustration is correct:

```
H. L. Wilson
2145 Valleyroad Avenue, South
Springfield, Missouri  65804




            Mr. Frank W. Whitfield
            118 Spring Street N. W.
            Atlanta, Georgia  30304
```

546 Appearance of the Business Letter. A business letter is usually typed on a sheet of paper 8½ by 11 inches. Double space is used between parts of the letter and between paragraphs. The typing should be so placed on the sheet as to have the margins properly proportioned, with the result that the typed space appears on the sheet much as does a picture properly set in a frame. Even when a letter conforms to all the other requirements of a good letter, its appearance is important. The indented form is often used in writing in longhand, but the block form is usual in typing (537A). The semiblock style, in which the paragraphs are indented (usually five spaces), is used by many business houses. The following letter is in the semiblock style:

126 Park Place
Torrance, California 90507
May 12, 19--

Mr. J. D. Foster
1770 Pearl Street
Denver, Colorado 80202

Dear Mr. Foster:

The information which you gave enabled me to obtain the Greeley contract which I had feared could not be concluded this spring. It was generous of you to take the trouble to assemble the data for me.

As soon as I have rechecked the specifications, I will see you for final details. You will agree with me, I know, that the outlook is promising for us.

Unless I meet with some unexpected delay, I should have this preliminary work completed by the end of the week. I will let you know the day and the hour to expect me.

Sincerely yours,

L. W. Whitman

L. W. Whitman

LWW:pb

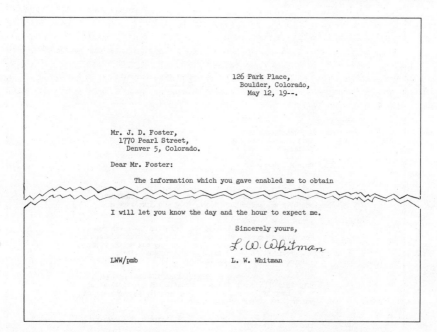

126 Park Place,
Boulder, Colorado,
May 12, 19--.

Mr. J. D. Foster,
1770 Pearl Street,
Denver 5, Colorado.

Dear Mr. Foster:

The information which you gave enabled me to obtain

I will let you know the day and the hour to expect me.

Sincerely yours,

L. W. Whitman

LWW/pmb   L. W. Whitman

547 Common Types of Business Letters. There are business letters appropriate to all phases of business; therefore it would be almost impossible to classify all types. Only the commonly used types can be discussed in a brief work such as this. The following types of business letters are common: **application, order, inquiry and reply, recommendation, introduction, claim, adjustment, acknowledgment and appreciation, collection, congratulation, sales.**

547A Application. The letter of application should conform to all requirements of a good business letter (536), and in form (536-546) it should be correct in every detail. No one should do less than his very best in writing a letter of application, for it is in reality a sales letter (547K) in which the writer is trying to sell his services. A short application letter may consist of three or four paragraphs. The first may mention the source of information about the position, the second may give facts that indicate one's qualifications for holding the position, the third may list references, and the fourth may suggest a possible conference or further communication. But even the conventional form of application may be altered to suit the originality of the writer and the type of position sought. The more individual the message, providing it is always sincere and sensible, the more evident the fitness to fill a position requiring originality.

```
                                   1735 Magnolia Avenue
                                   Dallas, Texas  75201
                                   October 10, 19--



           Mr. John Hamilton
           1917 Houston Street
           Dallas, Texas  75201

           Dear Mr. Hamilton:

               I have just learned from Mr. Jones, one of your
           salesmen, that you wish to employ a reliable boy to help
           with deliveries and to do odd jobs about the store after
           school hours and on Saturdays.  I should like very much
           to have you consider me for this work.

               I am fourteen years old and am now in the ninth grade.
           For three summers I have been with the Gray Drug Company as
           delivery boy and general helper.  You may ask Mr. H. W. Gray,
           the president of this company, about my qualifications.  His
           telephone number is 283-8142.

               Also, I refer you to Principal H. G. White of Lowell
           High School, where I am now a student, and to Principal
           W. B. Lake of Roosevelt Junior High School, the school from
           which I was transferred last January.

               I should be very happy to talk with you.  My telephone
           number is 314-3657.

                                   Yours very truly,

                                   Harold Roberts

                                   Harold Roberts
```

547B   Order. The letter ordering goods should be made so clear that it could not possibly be misunderstood. It should be exact and complete in every detail as to quantity, quality, size, catalogue number, shape, style, color, prices, or other item (use sample of paper, cloth) helping toward exact identification. If the buyer is to pay transportation charges, he should specify how the order is to be shipped—mail, express, or freight—unless he leaves this matter to the one who ships. Give complete instructions for shipping. Printed order blanks may be used, but in any case few words should be written in addition to those giving the items and exact instructions relative to the order. Write each item on a separate indented line. If payment is enclosed, state the exact amount and the form in which it is sent—stamps, currency, check, draft, or money order. An enclosure may be stapled to the letter, but paper clips should be avoided. In the lower left-hand corner should be written *Enclosure, Encl.,* or *Enc.*

Madison High School   Hicksville, New York 11802

January 10, 19--

McCormick-Mathers Publishing Company, Inc.
1440 East English
Wichita, Kansas 67201

Gentlemen:

Please send me the following books and the tests and
other materials that accompany them by freight, shipping
charges collect:

41 PLAIN ENGLISH 7 @ 57¢		$ 23.37
36 PLAIN ENGLISH 8 @ 57¢		20.52
32 PLAIN ENGLISH 9 @ 57¢		18.24
30 PLAIN ENGLISH 12 @ 42¢		12.60
109 PLAIN ENGLISH HANDBOOK-Paperbound @ 57¢		62.13
30 PLAIN ENGLISH HANDBOOK-Clothbound @ 1.71		51.30
68 ESSENTIALS IN ENGLISH, Third Book @ 93¢		63.24
		$251.40

Our check for $251.40 is enclosed.

Yours very truly,

J. D. Price

JDP:mb   J. D. Price, Principal
Enclosure

547C   Inquiry and Reply. The letter of inquiry should make absolutely
clear the information wanted. It should leave no possibility of the
recipient's having to write to ask for explanation or extension of any
of its parts. It should be as brief as is in keeping with courtesy and
clarity. If the purpose of the inquiry is of no interest to the recipient,
a stamped, self-addressed envelope should be enclosed for reply.

One who receives an inquiry should reply promptly unless it is a type of inquiry out of keeping with business ethics. Even when the purpose of the inquiry is of no interest to the recipient, he should give the information as courteously and as fully as if it meant material profit to him. He should give not only complete information for every detail of the inquiry but also any additional information which he feels would be of help in the situation. In short, the writer should send just the kind of reply he would wish if he were the inquirer.

L. W. STEVENS & SON

675 North Woodcock Road · Flint, Michigan 48522

July 8, 19--

Mr. Fred Warner
Warner Drug Store
2451 Northville Drive
Grand Rapids, Michigan 49505

Dear Mr. Warner:

    Mr. J. H. Webb has applied for work as salesman in my drugstore. He has referred me to you as one for whom he has done similar work. Please give me some general information as to his fitness for this work. I shall be grateful to you for this help.

Sincerely yours,

L. W. Stevens

L. W. Stevens

LWS-PMB

Answer to the letter on p. 110:

R̸x   **Warner Drugstore**

2451 Northville Drive   Grand Rapids, Michigan   49505

July 9, 19--

Mr. L. W. Stevens
L. W. Stevens and Son
675 North Woodcock Road
Flint, Michigan 48502

Dear Mr. Stevens:

    Mr. J. H. Webb worked for me two years, and I found him
thoroughly dependable and efficient all the time. You may be
sure that he will give you excellent service. It was very
difficult for me to find a salesman of his ability to replace
him when he moved to your city. I shall appreciate any consideration you show him.

              Yours sincerely,

              Fred Warner

FW/ss   Fred Warner

547D Recommendation. The letter of recommendation may be either
personal or general. The personal type, such as the letter of reply
just above, is addressed to a person or firm by a writer who is recom-
mending someone for a position. It may be written at the request of
the one seeking the position or in answer to inquiry of the prospec-
tive employer. It should give definitely and clearly the information
which would help the employer most in determining the applicant's
fitness for the position.

There should be no vague statements and no overstressing of good
qualities to make the applicant seem superhuman.

The general type of recommendation, which is placed in the hands of the one recommended, is not in favor at present and does not carry much weight because the tendency of the writer is to give only favorable facts. The employer of today prefers to send a questionnaire to references furnished by the applicant. In this way he gets information which might be omitted from the general letter of recommendation. Of course, he interprets failure of a reference to answer the questionnaire or any item of it as unfavorable to the candidate. The following, sent in answer to an inquiry, not containing a questionnaire, is an example of a longer recommendation than the preceding letter.

DOWELL INSURANCE SERVICE
1622 White Avenue
Knoxville, Tennessee   37901

June 12, 19--

Mr. Henry Jones
Central Insurance Company
1668 Blair Street
Louisville, Kentucky 40201

Dear Mr. Jones:

It is with pleasure that we recommend Mr. F. H. Warren, about whom you inquire in your letter of June 10. He has been with us for five years and in that time he has continued to grow in efficiency as an insurance salesman until he is now among our largest and most consistent producers of quality business. It is because of this development that he now wishes to enter a larger field, such as you can offer him. We realize that his going will mean serious loss for us, but we do not wish to hold him back from the greater opportunities you can provide.

Mr. Warren is a persistent and tireless worker who considers rebuffs only as a challenge to lead him to improve his sales presentation. He is, we sometimes think, unduly impatient at his own reasonable progress; but this may be, after all, a commendable trait.

You will, we feel sure, find many occasions to consider yourselves fortunate if you engage Mr. Warren as a salesman.

Sincerely yours,

C. C. Dowell

CCD:ebe   C. C. Dowell, President

547E Introduction. The letter of introduction is used to introduce two of the friends or acquaintances of the writer. It may be given for either business or social reasons, but it should never be given except in all seriousness. One should never give a letter of introduction for business purposes unless one is absolutely sure of the ability and integrity of the person introduced. It would be much better to refuse to give the letter than to give less than full approval of the person or to run the risk of introducing one not thoroughly competent and reliable. The message should be simple and as brief as is consistent with completeness and courtesy. The letter, delivered in person by the one introduced, should be enclosed in an unsealed envelope, bearing in proper position the name and full address of the one for whom it is intended and in the lower left-hand corner the words *Introducing Mr. Blank.*

```
                              1846 Oak Street
                              Springfield, Missouri  65801
                              October 6, 19--




     Mr. F. L. Harper
     1720 Market Street
     St. Louis, Missouri  63155

     Dear Mr. Harper:

          This will introduce to you Mr. Clay Holton, who is
     seeking a position in your city.  I have known him all his
     life, and his training, ability, and integrity fit him for
     excellent service in business--the field in which he special-
     ized in the University of Missouri, from which he was gradu-
     ated last June.

          For whatever courtesy or favor you may show this young
     man, both he and I will be grateful to you.

                              Sincerely yours,

                              James K. Atherton

     JKA:AB                   James K. Atherton
```

547F Claim. A letter of complaint or claim should always be courteous, dignified, and fair. It should state exactly the cause for complaint and should outline clearly the reasonable adjustment expected. The complainant who imputes blame or becomes sarcastic or abusive only emphasizes his own lack of refinement and makes less probable the adjustment he seeks. If the writer gives the impression that he takes for granted that he is dealing with those who are absolutely honest and eager to make any reasonable adjustment, he will seldom fail to get satisfaction. If he has had previous satisfactory dealing with the company, it is well to mention it to substantiate his expressed confidence. Most companies are quick to respond favorably to a justified complaint.

```
                                        3636 Weldon Street
                                        Dallas, Texas  75201
                                        May 6, 19--




        The Glacier Book Company
        340 Vine Street
        Denver, Colorado  80202

        Gentlemen:

            On May the first I ordered from you one copy of
        Magic Mountain by Dale Warwick.  The book arrived by
        mail today, and I found that some of the pages were
        transposed so that the volume was not usable.  I should
        like the privilege of returning the defective book to
        you in exchange for a perfect copy.

            I shall wait for instructions from you.

            You may be sure that I will appreciate your adjust-
        ing the matter for me.

                                    Yours very truly,

                                    H. C. Bradford
                                    H. C. Bradford
```

547G Adjustment. The writing of the letter of adjustment sometimes calls for much diplomacy. Those who write letters of complaint often do so while they are angry or in a disagreeable mood, but those who answer them should do so in such a way as to promote good feeling. Even when the complainant is very unreasonable and abusive, a reply showing courtesy and fairness is usually most effective. When the requested adjustment is to be made, the letter may be quite simple. An apologetic tone should be avoided.

The GLACIER
BOOK CO. 340 Vine Street   Denver, Colorado   80202

May 8, 19--

Mr. H. C. Bradford
3636 Weldon Street
Dallas, Texas 75201

Dear Mr. Bradford:

    Thank you for calling our attention to the imperfect
copy of Magic Mountain. We regret that you have been caused
inconvenience, and we assure you that we are glad to adjust
the matter. We are sending you by parcel post another copy
of the work, and we are enclosing with this letter postage
for the return of the imperfect volume.

    We appreciate this opportunity of making our service
satisfactory, and hope to continue to be of service to you
in the future.

                              Very truly yours,

                              L. W. Glade

LWG:EBK   L. W. Glade
Encl.   President

547H   Acknowledgment. The receipt of an order or a remittance should be acknowledged at once. If the acknowledgment is of an order, it should refer to the date of the order with other definite reference to identify it clearly. It should state when and how the order is to be shipped, and detailed explanation should be given if there is to be any delay in filling the order.

Frequently a customer has ordered without adequate information about the differences in products available for shipment, which the acknowledgment must explain. If the order lacks necessary details, such as sizes or other specifications, the writer of the acknowledgment should refer to the omission without showing impatience. In short, the acknowledgment should reflect sincere appreciation and should foster a spirit of good will. An acknowledgment of remittance should be made promptly, and always it should express that sincere appreciation which encourages further business relations. It often has elements of the sales letter (547K). The following is an example of the **letter of acknowledgment.**

BOVELL Sporting Goods Company

207 Kenworth Road   Columbus, Ohio   43214

March 3, 19--

Mr. Robert Leewright
325 Central Drive
Lancaster, Pennsylvania 17601

Dear Mr. Leewright:

Thank you for your order of February 27 for our X214--
7½-ft. spinning rod and L-340 spinning reel with 200
yards of 6-pound-test monofilament line. These will be
shipped to you by express prepaid today.

You asked about our automatic reel A160 for fly rods.
This will easily hold 25 yards of GAF line, but not 35
yards as you specify. May I suggest our A260 Automatic
Reel, described in the enclosed circular? This is one
of the finest reels on the market and has proved very
popular. I believe it would fill the needs you indicate
in your letter. The circular contains a convenient order
form for your use.

Your order is very much appreciated, and we hope that
we may continue to be of service to you.

Very truly yours,

Norman Roberts

NR:RM   Norman Roberts
Encl.   Sales Manager

5471 Collection. The writer of the successful collection letter must use tact. He has the difficult task of collecting the money and of retaining the good will and continued patronage of the customer. Therefore, he must not use a tone that will offend the customer. With all his courtesy and consideration, however, he must not leave the impression that he is easygoing. He should not be too friendly or too sympathetic; and, above all, he should not be apologetic. Firmness should always be apparent.

oods department store

MAIN AT MERRITT   RACINE, WISCONSIN 53401

May 12, 19--

Mr. J. F. G----
615 West Fifth Avenue
Spokane, Washington 99210

Dear Mr. G----:

What do you think we should do?

We have a small account that remains unpaid. We have sent two reminders. We are sincerely interested in keeping the good will of all our customers; yet we cannot continue to build up a large collection expense. What would you suggest that we do?

This small account is yours. It is only $46.28, but it is six weeks overdue. You know the value of your credit privilege, and I am sure you want to retain it. Our spring sales will soon place a wide selection of fine bargains on our shelves, and you will find your credit with us a valuable convenience.

Our extension of time on your account has already been most liberal. In justice to our other customers and as a matter of fair play, won't you settle this account at once and retain your good credit standing?

I am enclosing an addressed, postage-free envelope for your convenience. Please make use of it now to send us your check. It will be appreciated.

Sincerely yours,

Olin Hiebert

OH:mr   Olin Hiebert
Enc.   Credit Manager

547J Congratulation. The message of congratulation in business need not be restricted by mere commercial relationships. It may be prompted more by courtesy than by obligation and it calls for no reply. It is of course very similar to the congratulatory letter of friendship (548F), but it should follow the business-letter form, and its tone is often more formal, depending on the personal relationships involved. The following message is an example of this type of letter.

McCORMICK-MATHERS PUBLISHING Co., INC.

P.O. BOX 2212 W I C H I T A , K A N S A S *67201*

EDITORIAL OFFICES • 55 Fifth Avenue, New York, New York 10003

October 18, 1961

Mr. Joseph R. Smith
4903 Ellis Avenue
Chicago, Illinois 60607

Dear Mr. Smith:

As soon as I heard of your election to the board of directors of your firm, I felt I must write you to let you know how happy I am in your advancement.

All of your friends have felt that, in spite of the great difficulties you have faced in your climb up through the ranks, the outstanding ability we all recognized in you could not go unacknowledged. This advancement is certainly your due, and I think your firm should also be congratulated on taking advantage more fully of your exceptional talents.

Sincerely yours,

Emil Holgerson
President

CEH:mr

547K **Sales.** The sales letter is generally considered not only the most important of all business letters but also the most difficult to write. The requirements of the business letter vary with individual types, but every good sales letter should accomplish these four things: **attract attention, arouse desire, secure conviction,** and **induce action.** To do these things best, it should conform to all requirements of the business letter (536B). The opening sentence in a sales letter should attract the attention of the reader and cause him to continue reading.

Wimberly's Grill

359 NORTH MAIN   **WICHITA, KANSAS 67202**

April 14, 19--

Mr. Gerald F. Bovell
1550 Fairmount Avenue
Wichita, Kansas 67206

Dear Mr. Bovell:

Do you eat to live or live to eat?

Either way, you will enjoy eating at Wimberly's. It goes
without saying that the food is exceptionally fine. Only
the choicest meats and produce enter our kitchen, and we
have long been famous for the preparation of our foods.
Have you ever tasted our spare ribs? Try them--you've
never tasted anything so delectable.

Then, too, you'll enjoy the efficient friendly service at
Wimberly's, the quiet decor, the pleasant atmosphere.

Why not come in for lunch or dinner today? We'll be glad
to see you and we promise you the best meal in town at a
very modest price.

Sincerely yours,

Robert Wimberly

Robert Wimberly
Manager

RW:lr

Social Correspondence

548   Social Letters. The social letter varies from the informal letter of friendship to the most formal note. Social letters may be divided into these groups: letters of **friendship, courtesy, formality.**

548A   Letters of Friendship. The letter of friendship may be light or dignified, and its style should be conversational (550A). Even the form is less conventional than that of the business letter, and the stationery may vary more to suit the taste of the writer. However, the general make-up is similar to that of the business letter, except that the **inside address** (538) may be placed at the left side three spaces below the signature. The **heading** (537), **salutation** (539), **complimentary close** (543), **signature** (544), **and outside address** (545) are similar to those of the business letter. Because the letter of friendship is usually written in longhand, many writers prefer to use the indented form (537A) in the letter parts. The punctuation (537B) of the parts is the same as for the business letter, except that a comma (instead of a colon) follows the salutation. The salutation, complimentary close, and signature are not so formal; these should be in keeping with the relationship of the correspondents. Such salutations as the following are appropriate: *Dear Fred, Dear Mr. Hilton, Dear Aunt Mary.*

Informal note of friendship:

> 6188 Maple Street
> Dallas, Texas 75201
> May 25, 19—

Dear Ruth,

   Why don't you write? Of course, you're busy with the close of school so near; but do take time to assure me that you will be here for my birthday. You have a standing invitation to attend all my birthday celebrations, and this is to warn you not to fail to attend this one. Mother says that you must stay at least two weeks—and Mother must be obeyed.

   Don't forget your tennis racket. The court is better than ever this spring. Don and Ted pronounce it "better than perfect" because they have done the perfecting. And by way of warning: Ted slings a mean racket this year—so you'd better be in practice. He plays rings around me.

   As I write, Skippy is cutting capers all around the room. I have just told him that I am writing to you and that you are coming soon. He's laughing now as he recalls running away with your tennis shoe that day. He was just a puppy then. He's almost grown up now, but he still has a weakness for tennis shoes.

Please write immediately (or earlier) to tell me when to park the family bus at the station. I must run now, or be late to English class.

Your pal,

Betts

P.S. There go Mary Lu and that "Robert Taylor" I told you about in my last letter. I do believe they're holding hands. No, it's my mistake. There's still a chance for you—if you hurry.

Reply to preceding informal invitation:

1122 Maple Wood
Houston, Texas 77002
May 27, 19—

Dear Betts,

It's a shame that business has kept me from answering your last letter. Your note makes me feel guilty, and I pause in my mad rush to say—hold everything (including the "Taylor" man) till that streamliner pauses at your station at half-past five next Saturday afternoon. Tell your mother I may not "obey" in full, but that I'll make her glad to be rid of me. As for Ted, say I'm out of practice—but unafraid. Warn Skippy that I'll show him a dog's life for a few days.

I'm five minutes late—but I'll make that committee meeting.

Good-by till Saturday.

Ruth

There are some points of the informal letter on which writers are not agreed. For instance, some omit the inside address altogether while others place it at the left below the signature; some even omit the heading. These are minor points which the individual must settle for himself.

548B   Letter of Courtesy. The letter of courtesy, as defined by Dr. Thomas Arkle Clark in his *When You Write a Letter* (Benj. H. Sanborn & Co.), is "the letter written not in reply to another letter nor yet to elicit a reply of any sort, but simply as an act of politeness and thoughtfulness to acknowledge a kindness or an obligation or to let one's friends or acquaintances know that one was aware of their sorrows and their successes, of their comings and goings, and that one had a real personal interest in these." Of the many classes of this type of letter only these four will be discussed: **acknowledgment, appreciation, condolence,** and **congratulation.**

548C   Acknowledgment or Thanks. There are many types of acknowledgment (547H) which duty and courtesy demand of us. It is obligatory that we acknowledge receipt of a letter, a present, an unusual courtesy, a favor, an offer, a request, or an invitation. There are many persons, however, especially youngsters, who do not respond to this obligation. They should know, though, that this failure of acknowledgment brands them as thoughtless or ungrateful.

Rosedale, California
July 15, 19—

Dear Mrs. Moore,

You may be sure that I shall always continue to enjoy the week which I have just spent in your home with Louise. You did everything possible to make us happy. The parties, the picnics, and the lunches were all so delightful and gay that I can never thank you enough for all the trouble you took for us.

Mother and I are already counting the days until Louise will be here with us. Tell her that I will write to her tomorrow.

Gratefully yours,

Mildred Mason

548D   Appreciation. There is perhaps no other form of letter which has greater possibilities of bringing joy to both writer and recipient than the letter of appreciation. Yet it is a type which is neglected, because we human beings seem more inclined to condemn than to praise. Dr. Clark (see 548B) says, "When there is something which can be criticized adversely or found fault with we jump at it with alacrity, but when we meet something worthy of praise, we say nothing." The expression of appreciation should be simple and sincere, with no inclination to flattery.

80 Federal Street
Boston, Massachusetts 02109
October 24, 19—

Dear Miss Webster,

Years ago when I was in your class in English, I became discouraged. You will never know just how discouraged I was when you came to my rescue. You saw hope for me when I knew only despair. You gave me renewed faith in myself, and I am writing now, after all these years, to thank you. But in my heart I have thanked you a million times, and now I wish you to know that to you I owe the success which I am enjoying.

In this mail I am sending you an autographed copy of my latest book, which is having a very good sale, and I wish you to remember as you read it that without your encouragement it would never have been written.

Gratefully yours,

Charles G. Martin

548E   Condolence. A letter of condolence (sympathy) should be written in longhand. It should always be short and must be sincere in tone. Avoid reference to death or sorrow. Usually, there is no occasion for a letter of condolence from young people. Letters sent by one's parents are usually adequate. At times a young person may feel the need to send some expression of his own feelings in a simple note such as the following:

Dear Fred:

My deepest sympathy goes to you in the loss of your mother. I shall always remember how friendly and encouraging she was to me when I came over to your house.

Most sincerely,

Tom

Also one person may be selected to write a letter of condolence for a group or class:

Dear Mrs. Smith:

The ninth grade has asked me to express to you our deepest sympathy and the feeling of loss we all have. Fred was a valued companion to all of us and we feel privileged to have known him.

Most sincerely,

Henry Jones

Class President

548F   Congratulation. Sincere, appropriate words at times of successful achievement make for greater happiness in both the business and social world (see also 547J):

356 Cochran Road
Lexington, Kentucky 40501
February 20, 19—

Dear Fred,

Your winning first place against such strong competition did not surprise me at all, but it did make me happy. I congratulate you, for I know it was hard work, not luck, that brought you victory.

Now that you have won first place in oratory in competition with representatives of the leading universities in the United States, I wonder if those of that smart set would still brand you hillbilly, as they did when they tried to rule you out of that first contest. If you are a hillbilly, you are running true to form, for there have been other Kentucky hillbillies (seems to me one was called "Abe") who have been heard from.

If I did not know you as I do, I'd offer some advice about disposing of your old hat. But I know it still fits you—you are immune from swelled head. You'll have to let me strut a little, though; I don't know any better.

Sincerely yours,

Jack

548G Formal Invitation, Acceptance, Regret. The formal invitation is always written in the third person. It has neither heading, inside address, salutation, complimentary close, nor signature. Only a few abbreviations such as *Mr., Mrs.,* and *Dr.* are permitted. Numbers other than street numbers are written out. The response to the invitation must be written in the same rigid form and must contain the information given by it.

Invitation:

Mr. and Mrs. Henry L. Black
request the pleasure of
Miss Mildred Ware's
company at dinner
on Wednesday evening, the fourth of June
at seven o'clock
421 Glendale Road

Acceptance:

Miss Mildred Ware
accepts with pleasure
Mr. and Mrs. Henry L. Black's
invitation for dinner
on Wednesday evening, the fourth of June
at seven o'clock

Regret:

Miss Mildred Ware
regrets that a previous engagement
prevents her accepting
Mr. and Mrs. Henry L. Black's
invitation for dinner
on Wednesday evening, the fourth of June
at seven o'clock

548H Telegrams. The telegram should be as brief as is consistent with clearness, which is absolutely essential. Telegrams are expensive, and every word over the minimum increases the cost; but the elimination of words at the expense of clearness is poor economy.

In all telegrams the date, address, and signature are sent without charge. Each word, long or short, is counted. Therefore it is economy to use one long word when it conveys the idea of two or more short ones. Punctuation marks are sent free. The word *stop* may be used between sentences, but is counted as one word each time it is used. A standard abbreviation like *C.O.D.* is counted as one word. When figures or mixed groups of figures, letters, and signs (as 65%) are used, each group of five is counted as one word.

MUST SELL PROPERTY BY NOON TOMORROW.
PLEASE WIRE OFFER BY THEN.

Newspaper Writing

549 **Newspaper writing** includes news stories, headlines, feature stories, interviews, editorials, announcements, syndicated columns, and miscellaneous articles.

549A **News Story.** The news story tells recent important or interesting events. It usually begins with a summarizing paragraph called the lead, which should answer most of these questions: *Who? What? When? Where? Why? How?* This paragraph should be accurate and concise, and it should contain the main facts so that the reader need not proceed further unless he wishes the details, which are given in the order of their importance in the paragraphs following the lead. Some newspapers are beginning to break away from the conventional lead.

549B **Suggestions for Writing News.**

1. Accuracy is of first importance. Get all the facts right. Be especially careful to write names accurately.

2. Tell the story simply. Use specific rather than general terms. Do not use unnecessary words.

3. Tell facts only, never the reporter's opinions.

4. In quoting, use the exact words of the person quoted. Never quote anything which would indicate ignorance on the part of the speaker unless there is a justifiable reason for doing so. In short, one should use tact and common sense in writing news just as in other forms of writing.

5. In preparing copy, follow exactly the instructions provided by the editor. A newspaper usually has a style sheet which tells which of certain alternative correct spellings and forms of capitalization and punctuation have been selected for the paper.

549C   Headlines. Headlines tell the news in a few words and guide the reader in finding the news he wishes to read. The main facts of the story should be emphasized in the headlines. Short words are preferable. Do not use *a, an,* and *the.* A headline writer must count the letters in each line he writes and rewrite it until he has made it the length specified in the style sheet of his newspaper. The large headlines contain several sections, each of which is called a **deck.** The top deck tells the most important fact. Each deck should have a verb, and should never end with a preposition. The present tense (186) and the active voice (179) are preferable.

549D   Feature Story. The feature story includes a variety of types other than the usual news stories; it may be a brief human-interest story suggested by some event introduced as news, or a fashion forecast, or a review; or it may be a long, informative article such as those that appear in Sunday magazine sections. The reporter may use a more individual style in writing feature stories than in reporting news and may sometimes state his own impressions and feelings or use quotations. Feature stories are frequently distinguished by headlines different from those used for news stories, or they may be printed in boxes.

549E   Report of Interview. One who intends to report an interview (see 550G) should have clearly in mind the questions he wishes to ask. He should ask these questions tactfully and should remember accurately the answers for later recording. As few notes as possible should be taken in the presence of the one interviewed, but the report should be written immediately after the interview. In the lead of such a story, a quotation from the one interviewed may be used. Also, his name should be featured as well as some of his characteristics. The subject of the interview or its purpose should likewise be featured.

549F   Editorials. An editorial is an essay (549P) on some subject of interest to the public. Each writer is free to use his own individual style. The editorial usually has a title instead of headlines and a lead. Its purpose is generally to present an argument, to entertain, or occasionally to give information. The argumentative type is usually on a subject of public interest and is often a plea for some reform. The facts upon which such an argument is based should be carefully verified by reliable authorities. The type which means to entertain is often a kind of informal essay and is usually less serious than the other forms, being sometimes satirical or humorous.

The Birthday of Will Rogers

THIS is the birthday of one of the most beloved figures in all American history—Will Rogers. Unexpected tragedy took him from the scene of public life at the height of his activity and the pinnacle of his fame but had he lived to be a hundred or more he would have retained a warm spot in the hearts of millions of Americans.

Will was born, according to his own statements, at Oolagah, Indian Territory, but it was Claremore, Okla., that gained fame as his home town and Claremore has completed a shrine to its most famous son.

Will was listed in *Who's Who* as a humorist, but he was far more than that. He was a philosopher, a counsellor, a guide to millions of Americans who depended upon his daily bit of philosophy or whimsical humor to set them right with the world. Will had the faculty of pointing the way to the truth in a kindly way.

A sudden mishap of the air snuffed out the lives of Will Rogers and Wiley Post, another famous son of Oklahoma, up in the wilds of Alaska. Numerous monuments were raised in his honor, even before the completion of the memorial at Claremore but the greatest memorial is the niche the cowboy humorist of Oklahoma still retains in the hearts of millions.

—Wichita *Beacon*

549G   Announcements. A form of writing for publication which is important but not extensive is the announcement, which should be brief, clear, emphatic, and free from exaggeration.

The Research Paper

549H   Source Material. Choose a subject in which you are interested and which is not too broad. Once you have chosen your subject, consult the card catalog and Readers' Guide in your library to find out what reference material is available. Notice the copyright date; some material may be out of date.

Keep in mind the difference between original and secondary sources of material. For example, in writing about a person, his letters would be an original source of information, and a printed collection of his letters would generally be almost as good as an original source (remember, however, that letters are sometimes edited). A secondary source would be the opinions of another author about the person under discussion. For important papers, original sources should be used when available.

5491 **Source Cards.** List each source on a separate card—usually 3 by 5 inches. Include—

1. **Author's name,** last name first, or the editor's name followed by the abbreviation *Ed.* If no author is given, list the title first.
2. **Title.** Underline the title of a book, magazine, or newspaper and put quotation marks around the title of an article or chapter.
3. **Publication data.** With book titles include the city where published, name of publisher, and copyright date.
4. **Library call number.** For books include the call number so that you don't have to look this up again. Here are samples of source cards for a book, an article in a magazine, and an article in an encyclopedia:

> 629.1 Beard, R.B., and Rotherham, A.C., *Space Flight and Satellite Vehicles,* New York: Pitman Publishing Corporation, 1958
>
> B36

> Posin, D.Q., "Eye on Space," *Popular Mechanics,* Vol. 111, May 1959, pp. 70-71

> "Space Travel," *The World Book Encyclopedia,* 1959 edition, Vol. 15, pp. 7610-7610 l

549J   **Outlines.** Start with a working outline showing clearly the topics you expect to write about. As you gather material, you may want to change this outline, omitting topics about which you find little source material and adding others that appear to be interesting or significant. After you have gathered all your information, you may make your final outline (529) to guide your writing.

549K   **Taking Notes.** The best way to gather material is to take notes on 3 by 5 inch or larger cards for which you have a file box. These cards will enable you to organize your material and refer readily to your information on each topic as you write. The following are helpful rules for taking notes:

1. **Use a separate card for each note.** This permits you to file your cards under the proper topic. Sometimes more than one card will be necessary for a topic.

2. **Take thorough notes on all of the points you hope to cover.** Many students find that three or four good notes are required for every page of the research paper. Don't keep repeating information even if it is found in different books, and don't take notes on material you don't plan to use.

3. **List the topic the note refers to.** Usually the topic is shown at the top left corner of the card. This enables you to refer to your notes quickly as you write and helps you to organize your material.

4. **Be accurate.** Your notes must report facts, figures, opinions, and quotations accurately. Double-check every word and every figure with your source. Give enough detail so that you yourself can understand what you have written.

5. **Mark each direct quotation clearly.** Put quotation marks around each short quotation. Longer quotations are shown by leaving larger margins (489). Take down the exact words, punctuation, and capitalization. Use three dots to indicate the omission of parts of a quotation (467). Use direct quotations only if you plan to give the exact opinion of an authority or if the same idea cannot possibly be expressed in your own words. Too many quotations will make a very weak paper. Express your own ideas in your own way.

6. **Identify the source and give the page reference for each note.** This information will be necessary for your footnotes (549M) and your bibliography (549N). You should have some key for connecting your note card with its source card. You may make up your own abbreviation for each source card, or you may number your source cards in order and then put the proper source number on each note card.

549L   **Writing the Paper.** If you have your purpose and viewpoint clearly in mind, you may start by writing an introduction. Otherwise, save your introduction to the last and start with your first topic. Follow your final outline in arranging your notes. In this way your material will be logically organized, but you still must supply transitions (522)—sometimes in whole paragraphs—to make your paper a unified, coherent whole. Try to make your sentences sound smooth and connected, not like a miscellaneous assortment of sentences hastily thrown together. A first draft may be written rapidly, but be very careful of the mechanics of your writing in your revised final copy.

549M Footnotes. General information—such as you have found in a number of different books—usually doesn't have to be credited. But specific information—statistics, direct quotations, opinions of experts—should be credited. You can give credit in two ways. If the source is clear, you may mention it briefly in a sentence within your paragraph: "As H. C. Lodge says in *Science* for May 22, 1959, . . ." But usually a footnote is best for complete reference to your source. At the end of material to be credited, put a number slightly above the line to correspond to the number you will use for your footnote at the bottom of the page. Numbers should usually run consecutively throughout your entire paper, but you may start over with each new page.

Material to be credited should be taken accurately from your note cards, and you can take from your source cards all the data necessary for your footnote credit. The following are examples of forms you may use for articles and books. Since you will have a full bibliography, you may omit publication data from your footnotes if your teacher approves.

Magazine article

[1] E. M. Shoemaker, "Moon Close Up," <u>National Geographic Magazine</u>, Vol. 126, November 1964, pp. 690-707

Encyclopedia article

[2] "Space Science and Exploration," <u>Collier's Encyclopedia</u>, 1964 edition, Vol. 21, pp. 343-380

Book

[3] Robert Wells, <u>Electronics, Key to Exploring Space</u>, New York: Dodd, Mead & Co., 1964, p. 125

When you refer several times to the same source, it is not necessary to repeat the entire footnote. Suppose you need to credit an article the second time before you refer to any other source. Simply write

Ibid. (meaning "in the same place") as your footnote, adding a page number if the page is different:

[4]Ibid., p. 71

Some writers use *Loc. cit.* when the page number is the same. If another footnote has intervened, write the author's name and *op. cit.* ("in the work cited"), or just use the author's name:

[5]Wells, op. cit., p. 71   [5]Wells, p. 71

If the author is not given, a shortened reference to the previous source may be used:

[6]Collier's Encyclopedia, p. 352

549N   Bibliography. At the end of your research paper give a bibliography of all the printed material you have used in preparing your paper. Usually your bibliography will include the same works that you credited in your footnotes, but you may list additional helpful works that you consulted but did not have to credit. The form of your bibliographical entries is the same as that in your source cards. These should be alphabetized and copied accurately.

> Shoemaker, E. M., "Moon Close Up," National Geographic Magazine, Vol. 126, November 1964, pp. 690-707

> "Space Science and Exploration," Collier's Encyclopedia, 1964 edition, Vol. 21, pp. 343-380

> Wells, Robert, Electronics, Key to Exploring Space, New York: Dodd, Mead & Co., 1964

Writing Essays

549P   Essays. The term *essay* is rather broad, for it includes all forms of short creative writing inspired by personal reactions. The inexperienced writer, however, should restrict his attempts at essay writing to one type—the informal, or familiar, essay. This form is the expression of the writer's own thoughts on his chosen subject. The subject and the style of the informal essay may vary to suit the writer. The style of the writing, though, is in keeping with the mood of the theme. Some suggestions offered for writing the informal essay follow: *make your reader share your ideas and understand their relation, choose appropriate words, use a simple style, use quotations and figures of speech, vary your sentences, revise for clearness and effectiveness.*

ORAL COMMUNICATION

550   Oral communication is made up largely of conversation, the most informal of the types of communication; but it includes speaking in public, which may vary greatly in degree of formality.

Conversation

550A   Conversational language is usually less formal than that which is written, even in letters; but the conversationalist meets with dangers not encountered by the writer. Here are some suggestions for those who would like to be good conversationalists:

1. **Be a good listener.** Perhaps there is no more effective way of gaining the reputation of being a good conversationalist than by listening attentively. So, be alert, and never interrupt.

2. **Get the other's viewpoint.** Do your best to see things as the other person sees them. This is not easy, but it is important.

3 **Learn the other person's interests.** Show interest in the other's interests, not just your own.

4. **Respect the opinions of others.** Though you may not agree with another in his opinions, respect them just the same.

5. **Never argue.** There is nothing to gain by argumentation in ordinary conversation, but there is much to lose.

6. **Make no reference to the other person's weakness.** Let him feel that you think him strong.

7. **Acknowledge superiority in others.** Even unlearned people have traits of superiority. Let your attitude acknowledge this.

8. **Stimulate the other's feeling of importance.** Honestly and sincerely encourage the other's self-respect.

9. **Say the other person's name.** But be sure to use the name naturally and not as if for effect, and be doubly sure to pronounce it correctly. No one ever quite forgives anyone who mispronounces or misspells his name.

10. **Do not be a know-all.** Perhaps the most unpopular of all conversationalists is the know-all, the chap who tops every tale, no matter how tall—the fellow who has been everywhere and seen everything at its best and worst.

11. **Do not be gloomy.** Do not dwell on mournful or depressing incidents or predictions. Try at least to appear cheerful and hopeful.

12. **Do not be a cynic.** Refrain from expressing the views of a disparager—a doubter—a pessimist.

13. **Never be catty.** Those who make catty remarks cannot hope to have friends.

14. **Do not be overcorrect.** Use good but natural speech, and do not overdo correctness by becoming finicky about unimportant usages. In your community use the language of your community.

15. **Be genuinely courteous.** Be tactful and courteous always. In a group, make everyone feel at ease. Include everyone in your conversation, and do not talk over the heads of anyone present. Encourage those who are reticent. They are often the most interesting talkers.

16. **Be able to make correct introductions.** Everyone should be able to introduce himself and to introduce others properly and tactfully. Any good book on etiquette will serve to refresh one's memory on special points in introductions, but ordinarily one can easily remember that the boy is presented to the girl, the man to the woman, and the younger person to the older. John Jones may introduce himself to another by saying, "I am John Jones." He may introduce two others, a boy and a girl, by saying, "Mildred Gray, this is Bob Jones." If Bob is seated, he rises at the introduction and says, "How do you do?" Mildred may or may not offer to shake hands; she need not rise if seated. Usually boys, on being introduced, shake hands; but a boy does not offer his hand to a girl. The forms of introductions are more or less fixed, but not to the exclusion of informality.

Speaking Before an Audience

550B Few become professional public speakers, but there are occasions in the life of everyone when the ability to address an audience effectively is highly advantageous. General suggestions include those on the **appearance of the speaker**, the **voice**, the **language**, the **preparation of the speech**, and the **delivery**:

1. **Appearance of the Speaker.** The speaker should be neatly and appropriately dressed. In facing his audience, he should assume an air of dignity and poise. After a slight pause, through which he stands in an easy, natural position, he should begin his talk. He should look at his audience without special attention to individuals. He should become so much absorbed in his message that his hands and feet will not seem awkward appendages. If he uses notes, they should be typed on small cards, so that he may glance at them without attracting the attention of the audience to them.

2. **Voice.** The speaker should use natural tones and should speak loudly enough to be heard distinctly by all. If there is a microphone, speak directly toward it. The voice should be well modulated with no tendency toward monotonous singsong. Every word should be pronounced correctly (573) and clearly.

3. **Language.** Use good language in speaking before an audience, especially in giving a formal address before a dignified audience. In such an audience there are sure to be those who associate errors in speech with ignorance. In the less formal type of talk, of course, one should, as in conversation, use a style less dignified and precise. Surely one who addresses an audience of close friends should have something of the privilege of informal conversation in adding here and there, say, a bit of slang to give color to the expression. Tact, that great aid in all situations in life, is never more suitably employed than in the language of the public speaker. The speaker possessed of an adequate vocabulary, common sense, and tact can win any audience.

4. **Preparation of the Speech.** In preparing a speech, one usually has in mind to instruct, to convince, or to entertain. Accordingly every part of the speech should be appropriate to its purpose. It should also be appropriate to the occasion on which it is given and to the audience. The speaker should not memorize his address, though he should have it carefully outlined in notes. The outline should consist of an introduction, main message, and conclusion.

5. **Delivery of the Speech.** Be sure that your beginning is forceful. The first sentence often determines the whole effect of an address. Never begin a speech with an apology. No matter how poorly prepared you are, never apologize. If jokes are used, be sure they have a purpose and that they are appropriate. If you cannot tell a joke well, omit it. One butchered joke will spoil the effect of a good speech. Be sincere, and above all, be enthusiastic —enthusiasm is contagious. There is no excuse for droning out a lifeless speech, even in a good cause, for it always hurts the cause it should promote. Be sure to stop promptly when your message is ended. In making an announcement, be brief; but make sure your announcement is fully understood.

Other Oral Communication

550C   The Telephone. Only general suggestions for the use of the telephone may be offered here:

1. Be sure to exercise the same courtesy and consideration in using the telephone that you would if you were talking directly with the person. This means, of course, that the voice should be properly modulated and that there must be no indication of indifference, inattention, hurry, impatience, or annoyance.

2. Be alert, responsive, and courteous under even the most trying circumstances.

3. The person responsible for the telephone conversation should terminate it. Therefore it is impolite for the one called to conclude the conversation unless there is good reason for doing so.

4. Do not prolong a telephone conversation on trivial matters when someone is waiting to use the telephone.

5. Do not use a business telephone for prolonged visiting.

6. Do not use another's private telephone without asking permission.

7. Do not, by undue noise or otherwise, disturb one who is using a telephone.

8. Do not eavesdrop when someone is using the telephone. It is impolite to question one about something you happen to hear him say in a telephone conversation to another.

550D   Oral Book Report. The oral book report seems to be growing in popularity in clubs and other organizations outside the schools. Those who learn to make effective book reports in school may, therefore, find their training very useful in maturer years. There are few definite rules for making a book report, but the following suggestions are appropriate:

1. Explain something of the purpose of the book.

2. Tell something of the characters and the setting when reviewing fiction.

3. Compare the work with others of a similar nature.

4. You may read extracts, but they should be carefully selected and well read; otherwise do not attempt to read.

5. Explain why you do or do not like the book.

6. Use good English without being bookish. Make your report clear and enjoyable.

550E   Storytelling. Storytelling at its best is a fine art. Few of us, of course, become artists in this field; but everyone should learn to tell stories at least reasonably well. In addition to the suggestions offered under 550B, there are others which good story-tellers follow, such as these:

1. Plunge immediately into the story.

2. Give the events in their logical order.

3. Vary your sentence structure, and put life into your expression.

4. Suit your mood to that of the story, but remember that tactful humor is seldom inappropriate.

5. Make your conclusion strong—imagination will help you to an impressive close.

550F   Anecdotes. Everyone should learn to tell anecdotes well. A bit of artful humor lends tang to any conversation, and the effectiveness of the public speaker often depends on his skill at using appropriate anecdotes. Here are a few general suggestions:

1. The anecdote should be suited to the listeners and to the occasion.
2. It should be brief.
3. It should have a point, revealed only with the conclusion. Have clearly in mind the exact wording of your final sentence.
4. Use common sense in your selection of anecdotes.
5. Tell your anecdote *effectively* once, but don't repeat any part of it.
6. Don't suggest that maybe your audience has heard the story before.

550G Interview. An interviewer should introduce himself (if he is not already known to the person to be interviewed) and then make clear the purpose of the interview. If the interviewer is seeking a position, he should state his qualifications frankly, accurately, and confidently without seeming boastful. After an interview, the interviewer should thank the one interviewed, whether the outcome of the interview is favorable or not.

550H Discussion. Friendly, intelligent discussion is one of the most enlightening forms of communication. Your teacher will help you plan interesting discussions in class. There is no lack of excellent subjects for such discussion: community affairs, current events, a story, a play, a poem, or some popular book.

In a good discussion everyone is interested and everyone wants to talk. Everyone has studied the topic and has something to say. There will be strong opinions and perhaps some excitement. This is as it should be; a discussion should be fun and should lead to self-expression. This does not mean that loss of temper or rude interruptions are acceptable self-expression. Excitement does not excuse discourtesy. Loud argument and squabbles destroy discussion. The following are suggested rules for good discussion.

1. Choose a topic of real interest to the group.
2. Give everyone a chance to talk.
3. Listen to what others say so that you can contribute to the line of discussion. Avoid repeating what someone else has said.
4. Stick to the subject.
5. Don't interrupt.
6. Show respect for others' opinions, but don't be shy in expressing your own opinion.
7. Be courteous in correcting a statement you think is an error.
8. Don't argue about facts: look them up.

To make sure that everyone who wishes to talk has a fair chance, the group should have a chairman. The discussion may be largely informal, but each student should "address the chair"—that is, he should say "Mr. Chairman" and wait until the chairman speaks his name. This procedure avoids the unprofitable situation in which everyone tries to talk at once. A good chairman will also keep the speakers on the subject.

Above all, avoid such remarks as "That's stupid," or "It's perfectly idiotic to think that."

550I Giving Information. Everyone should train himself to ask for and to give information briefly, accurately, and courteously. In giving information, as for instance, on how to find a place, it is often necessary to repeat for emphasis; but too much repetition confuses.

550J Announcements and Brief Talks. Everyone should be able to make clear, effective announcements and to make creditable short talks before audiences. Every student should be able to announce effectively a coming event, make a rousing pep talk, introduce a speaker, make a nomination speech or a presentation speech. In all these one should remember to stick to the main purpose, be brief, give facts, and make a strong beginning and closing.

550K Clubs and Other Organizations. Work in organized groups in schools is so familiar to students of the present that detailed instructions are not needed here. You have, no doubt, taken part in many school organizations. Under the guidance of your teacher, you have become familiar with the working rules of groups. If there are points on which you are not clear, any standard work, such as R. M. Robert, *Robert's Rules of Order, Revised,* Scott, Foresman and Co., or A. Sturgis, *Sturgis Standard Code of Parliamentary Procedure,* McGraw-Hill Book Co., Inc., will set you right. A summary of the essential rules for regular club work would include these: *how to call a meeting to organize a group, how to nominate and elect officers, how to make a motion, how to second a motion, how to call a meeting to order, how committees are appointed, how the chairman of a committee is selected.* A knowledge of these rules coupled with good judgment and consideration for others will enable you to do effective, enjoyable club work.

Seven: CHOICE OF WORDS

STANDARDS OF DICTION

551 **Language is growing.** A living language is constantly changing. Its standards of correctness are established by those who are considered its most authoritative users. Inexperienced writers and speakers especially should stay within the limits of those standards and use only words which are sanctioned by best authority. However, this standard of correctness may vary with the form of expression in which it is found. The formal literary type of expression would be out of place in the more informal situation requiring a colloquial (555)* type of expression. The report of a football game kept to the standard required for a formal essay would no doubt be rather dull reading. Even the standard required for the less formal kinds of writing might be altogether out of place in conversation. **Good English is that which is appropriate to the type of expression in which it is used.**

Diction as used here refers to the choice of words for accuracy, clearness, variety, and effectiveness rather than to the manner of speaking.

VARIETIES OF DICTION

552 There are types of expressions which are avoided by the best writers and speakers. But there are other types of word usage that are perfectly acceptable when appropriate to the situation. An understanding of this appropriateness marks the educated person. Most types of word usage may be classified under the following headings: **archaic expressions, barbarisms, colloquialisms, improprieties, newly coined words, provincialisms, slang, vulgarisms, hackneyed or trite expressions,** and **idiomatic expressions.**

553 **Archaic Expressions.** Words are archaic which are old-fashioned, no longer used naturally: *spirituous* (for spirited), *eftsoons* (for *soon after*), *methinks, avaunt:*
    Archaic: The youthful crowd will be *convocated* here *anon.*
    Modern: The youngsters will *gather* here *soon.*

554 **Barbarisms.** Avoid word distortions, such as *alright, complected, disremember, irregardless.*
    Barbarism: I *disremember* the incident.
    Standard: I do not *remember* the incident.

* *Numbers in parentheses refer to sections of this book.*

555 Colloquialisms. Some expressions are correctly used in informal conversation or in informal writing but are not appropriate in formal composition. The ordinary contractions, such as *doesn't, hasn't,* and *can't,* are examples of colloquialisms. The modern colloquial style of writing requires skill.

Colloquial: It is *funny* that he *doesn't* return.

Formal: It is *strange* that he *does not* return.

556 Improprieties. Good words may be used inappropriately, such as *set* for *sit, most* for *almost, accept* for *except, affect* for *effect:*

Impropriety: It seems that *most* all the students are here.

Correct. It seems that *almost* all the students are here.

557 Newly Coined Words. Large numbers of words are added to the language or changed in meaning each year, and they are not necessarily to be avoided. When in doubt, check with an up-to-date dictionary.

Recently Coined: Fred wore his new *beanie* to school.

Jane will *baby-sit* for us tonight. (now widely accepted)

558 Provincialisms. Dialectal words, or provincialisms, are expressions peculiar to a locality, such as *carry* (for *accompany*),*poke* (for *bag* or *sack*), *cayuse* (for *range horse*), *jolt wagon* (for *farm wagon*).

Provincial: She cooked a meal in the *spider.*

More General: She cooked a meal in the *frying pan.*

559 Slang. Are you a square? Or is *square* (to describe a person) so outdated that you would call anyone who used it a "cord"? Both are terms of scorn; *square* is given in some dictionaries as a slang term to refer to a person who does not fit in with the "in" group; *cord* does not seem to have made the dictionary and may already have disappeared from teenage language. Most slang is quickly worn to threads, or it may change its meaning to the opposite of its original sense. *Cool* used to mean "the best"—now it may mean "the worst."

Slang may be the language of your group, but usually it would be smart not to use it in writing or in talking with older people. Adults may have at one time in their lives used a great deal of slang, but they know how tiresome and meaningless it may become. But sometimes slang is clever, forceful, or picturesque and may become part of the language of literature people. Such words as *sob story, mob,* or *stooge* are now generally accepted. Slang should not be entirely despised, but it should be used with care.

Some common slang terms are *okeydoke, goon,* (for *stupid person*), *real gone* (for *great*), *dig* (for *appreciate*).

Slang: She is a *lulu.*

Standard: She is a *wonderful person.*

560 Vulgarisms. Some words are never correct in either formal or informal expression, words such as *blowed, brung, busted, drawed, drowned, et, growed, hain't, hern, hisn, hisself, knowed, nowheres, scairt, theirn, theirselves, them there,* and *this here.* The term also applies to obscenities.

561 Hackneyed or trite expressions. Phrases which have been over-used until they have almost lost their effectiveness are **trite.** Although young writers are tempted to use these worn-out expressions, they should learn to substitute more vital ones. Some of the hackneyed terms frequently used are *brave as a lion, brown as a berry, busy as a bee, cold as ice, green as grass, pearls before swine.*

562 Idiomatic expressions. Idioms are expressions which are peculiar to a language, and often they are not governed by the rules of grammar; therefore it is difficult to translate them into another language. **Idioms,** though they may defy the laws of grammar, have nevertheless become through long-continued usage firmly established as standard.

That these expressions at first glance may not be parsed or diagrammed should not discourage their use. Our very best writers make frequent use of idioms. Some of the common idioms are *put up with, all of a sudden, get rid of it, in the long run, get into hot water, with a grain of salt.* Be careful to use correct idioms. The prepositions especially are often determined by idiomatic use rather than logic:

Unidiomatic: Hal was *accompanied with* his brother.
Correct: Hal was *accompanied by* his brother. (See 345.)

USAGE GLOSSARY

563 Some of the expressions listed here are in established use in **informal speech and writing,** but the standard here is for the **more formal expression in writing.** Remember, however, that usage changes. Learn to check with the dictionary.

564 Act. When used as a linking verb to mean "seem" or "pretend to be," *act* is followed by an adjective:

He certainly *acted* stupid.

Ad. This short form for *advertisement* is not an abbreviation and should not be followed by a period. It should not be used in formal writing:

Colloquial: I saw your *ad* in the paper.
Formal: I read your *advertisement.*

Affect—Effect. *Affect* is a verb meaning *influence* or *to pretend.* *Effect* as a verb means *to bring about; effect* as a noun means *result:*

The noise *affects* (not *effects*) my hearing.

They *effected* (not *affected*) a compromise.

His work had a good *effect* (not *affect*).

All right. There is no such word as *alright.* The word *alright* may appear in comic strips, but it suggests careless writing. Use the phrase *all right:*

Is it *all right* (not *alright*) to take the car?

All the farther. Do not use this expression for *as far as:*

This is *as far as* (not *all the farther*) I may go.

Already—all ready. *Already* is the adverb:

The guests had come *already.*

We were *all ready* for the fun.

Alternative. This means a *choice between two things.*

He had the *alternative* of resigning or being fired.

Altogether—all together. *Altogether* is the adverb:

This is *altogether* bad.

They were *all together* in the boat.

A one. It is superfluous to use *a* with *one* in a sentence like this:

There was not *one* (not *a one*) who would volunteer.

As. After verbs of *saying, knowing, thinking,* or *feeling,* do not use *as* for *whether* or *that* (369). (See also 362 and 372.)

I do not know *that* (not *as*) I can go.

In negative statements use the correlatives *so—as;* in positive statements use *as—as:*

He is not *so* tall *as* John.

He is *as* tall *as* John.

At. Do not use *at* unnecessarily:

Where is the book *at?* (Omit *at.*)

565 Awful. This term originally meant *awe-inspiring,* but it has been so weakened by its colloquial use that it can seldom be used with its original meaning. *Awful* and *awfully* should be avoided in most writing since they are merely general terms of emphasis or disapproval:

Jane is *unusually* (not *awfully*) beautiful.

This was a *difficult* (not an *awful*) job.

Badly. In formal writing do not use this term in the sense of *very much* or as a predicate adjective (280):

I want *very much* (not *badly*) to succeed.

He looks *bad* (not *badly*) since his illness.

Complected. This is a provincialism:

She is light-*complexioned* (not -*complected*).

Compliment—complement. A *compliment* expresses praise; a *complement* completes:

He paid her a charming *compliment*.

The verb has two *complements*.

Considerable. Do not use this term as a noun; use it as an adjective:

A *considerable* sum of money is invested in that plant.

566 **Credible—credulous.** *Credible* means *believable; credulous* means *believing too easily:*

That is a *credible* story.

He is too *credulous*.

Disremember. This word is frowned on, though marked *colloquial* in some dictionaries:

I *do not remember* (not *disremember*) his name.

Either—neither. Used to indicate one of two persons or things:

None (not *neither*) of the four boys would go.

Either of the two girls can take the part.

567 **Enthuse.** Although classed as *colloquial* by dictionaries, there is much prejudice against this word:

He is *enthusiastic* (not *enthused*) about the plan.

Expect. In formal writing do not confuse *expect,* meaning *to anticipate,* with *suppose,* meaning *to be of the opinion:*

I *suppose* (not *expect*) he is wealthy.

We *expect* to see you tomorrow.

Farther—further. The distinction between *farther* to refer to spatial distance and *further* to refer to time, degree, or quantity is waning, but some still observe it:

We walked *farther* than two miles.

I shall go no *further* with this business.

Fix. This is colloquial when used to mean *predicament, difficult situation,* or *condition:*

I was in a desperate *situation* (not *fix*) about my grades.

Formally—formerly. *Formally* means "in a formal manner"; *formerly* means "previously":

The guest was treated *formally*.

He was *formerly* mayor of the town.

Funny. Do not use for *odd* or *strange,* except in colloquial expressions:

It is *strange* (not *funny*) that he lost his fortune.

Gent. Should never be used for *gentleman.*

Gentleman—lady. These terms are sometimes applied to show respect but are often merely pretentious. The terms *man* and *woman* are best for general use:

I met a strange *woman* (not *lady*) on the road.

Get up. Should not be used for *organize, prepare,* or *arrange:*

They *prepared* (not *got up*) a good dinner.

568   **Good.** Do not use the adjective *good* as an adverb (320):

He sings *well* not *good*).

Got. *Got* is often used colloquially with *had, has,* or *have* to indicate possession or obligation emphatically. Avoid it in formal writing.

INFORMAL: I have *got* to go immediately.

Had ought to. *Do* not use *had ought to* for *ought to* or *should:*

You *ought* (not *had ought*) to write to Ned.

You *should* (not *had ought to*) read this book.

Imply—infer. A speaker or writer may *imply* more than he says; the hearer *infers* what the speaker intends:

We *inferred* from what Jim said that he was angry with us.

The speaker did not *imply* that anyone was to blame.

Invite—invitation. It is dialectal to use the word *invite* for the noun *invitation:*

She has an *invitation* (not *invite*) to the party.

Is where—is when. These terms should not be used in definitions:

Subtraction is *taking* (not *where you take*) one number from another.

569   **Kind of—sort of.** It is better not to use these terms for *rather* or *somewhat* (324):

She seems *rather* (not *sort of*) stupid.

Lay—lie. *Lay* is usually transitive and takes a receiver of its action; its principal parts are *lay—laid—laid. Lie* is intransitive in its usual meanings and does not take an object; its principal parts are *lie—lay—lain* (see 210):

Did you *lay* (not *lie*) the rake on the ground?

You should not *lie* (not *lay*) on the wet grass.

Learn—teach. *To learn* means to *get knowledge; to teach* means *to give knowledge* (220):

Teach me to swim.

You should *learn* to play tennis.

Less—fewer. *Less* refers to *quantity; fewer* refers to *number:*

This lake has *less* water than the other.

This tree has *fewer* branches than that.

Liable—likely. *Likely* means *probably; liable* means *responsible* or it may refer to a *possibility with unpleasant results:*

He is *likely* (not *liable*) to win the race.

He is *liable* to harm someone.

Like. In formal writing do not use *like* for *as* or *as if* in introducing a clause:

Do *as* (not *like*) I do.

He acted *as if* (not *like*) he knew.

Mad. Do not use *mad* for *angry* in formal situations:

John was *angry* (not *mad*) because of the delay.

Most. Do not use adjective *most* for the adverb *almost* (319):

We sold *almost* (not *most*) all the tickets.

Note that *almost* modifies indefinite pronouns: *almost everybody, almost anyone* (307).

570 **Nohow.** Should not be used as an adverb:

This machine won't run *at all* (not *nohow*).

None. This word has long been accepted as singular or plural:

None *were* pleased with the result.

None of the girls *was* present.

Off—from Do not use *off* or *off of* for *from:*

He bought the book *from* (not *off* or *off of*) me.

Off of. The *of* is unnecessary:

He jumped *off* (not *off of*) the car.

Party. Do not use for *person* except in terms of law:

I saw the *person* (not *party*) who won the prize.

Raise—rear. *Raise* is good informal usage for "bring up," but the following is formal:

They *reared* (not *raised*) three children.

He *raised* (not *reared*) hogs for market.

Raise—rise. In its usual meanings *raise* is transitive and takes a receiver of its action; its principal parts are *raise—raised—raised*. *Rise* is intransitive and almost never takes an object; its principal parts are *rise—rose—risen* (see 210):

The plane *rose* (not *raised*) quickly as it flew away.

Jim *raised* (not *rose*) the window.

571 **Real.** Avoid the adjective *real* for the adverbs *very* or *really* (302):

She is *very* (not *real*) attractive.

Reason. A statement containing *the reason is* is preferably completed by a *that* clause:

The reason he succeeded is *that* (not *because*) he worked hard.

Reverend, Honorable. Do not place a surname immediately after either of these terms: *The Reverend George Smith* (not *Reverend Smith*); *The Honorable Paul Miller.*

Set—sit. *Set* is usually transitive and takes a receiver of its action; its principal parts are *set—set—set*. *Sit* is intransitive in its usual meanings and does not take an object; its principal parts are *sit—sat—sat* (see 210):

Set (not *sit*) the chair in the corner.

We *sat* (not *set*) on the grass to rest.

So. Do not use it as an intensive in formal writing:

He is *extremely* (not *so*) careful.

572 **Suspicion.** Not in good use as a verb:

They *suspected* (not *suspicioned*) him of theft.

This here—that there. Omit *here* and *there*:

I like *this* (not *this here*) model.

To—at. Do not use *to* for *at* in such sentences as this:

He is *at* (not *to*) home now.

Wait on. Do not use for *wait for*:

Do not *wait for* (not *wait on*) me if my plane is late.

Ways—way. Use the singular form in sentences like this:

He rode a short *way* (not *ways*) with us.

Widow woman. Omit *woman*:

She is a *widow* (not *widow woman*).

Wire. Should not be used for *telegram* in formal writing:
I will send you a *telegram* (not *wire*) tomorrow.

Without no. Do not use this double negative (327):
He worked without *any* (not *no*) plans.

PRONUNCIATION

573 The only sure guide to correct pronunciation is a standard dictionary. *Webster's New Students Dictionary* has in the front a section on pronunciation, pages 9a to 20a, which gives extensive information on the subject. The words given below are some about whose pronunciation many people are uncertain:

abdomen	coupon	grimace	library
acclimate	creek	harass	literature
admirable	defect	hearth	maintenance
adult	despicable	height	mischievous
almond	detail	heinous	museum
apparatus	docile	horizon	paraffin
apricot	encore	hospitable	penalize
architect	exquisite	idea	pergola
athlete	finance	impotent	pumpkin
automobile	forehead	impious	quantity
bouquet	formidable	industry	recognize
chauffeur	gape	inquiry	research
chic	garage	interesting	sagacious
cognomen	genuine	irreparable	salmon
column	gondola	irrevocable	surprise
combatant	government	Italian	sword
comparable	granary	laboratory	vagary
condolence	gratis	lamentable	villain

FIGURES OF SPEECH

574 A **figure of speech** is a variation from the ordinary method of expression for the sake of effect. Though there are many figures of speech, the two in most common use are the **simile** and the **metaphor**. There are many other figures often used. Two of these are **personification** and **hyperbole**. Figures are employed effectively in both prose and poetry. Good examples of the use of the simile especially may be found in such familiar poems as Shelley's "To a Skylark" and Kilmer's "Trees."

574A A **simile** is a comparison, introduced by *like* or *as*, of two things which in their general nature are different from each other:
She is like a *beautiful flower*.

574B The **metaphor** is implied comparison. Instead of stating the comparison, as in the simile, the likeness is suggested by terms not literally applicable to each other:

She is a *beautiful flower*.

A *wave of emotion* overcame him.

574C Do not use **mixed metaphors,** such as these:

He is aflame with a thirst for knowledge.

Life is not all a rough sea; sometimes its pathway is smooth.

574D **Personification** is the figure of speech in which some human characteristic is attributed to an inanimate thing:

The *friendly* hills seemed to *welcome* us.

574E **Hyperbole** is exaggeration for the purpose of emphasis and without the intention of being taken literally:

I am *completely starved*.

SYLLABICATION

575 There are a few general rules which young writers should observe in dividing syllables. The following are important:

1. Place the hyphen at the end of the line when dividing syllables, not at the beginning of the next line.
2. Do not divide words having only one syllable, not even long words like *thought*.
3. In compounding two words, place the hyphen between them.
4. Be sure to divide words between syllables when division is necessary at the ends of lines.
5. Do not divide a word at the end of a line so that a single letter is separated from the rest of the word: *ra-dio*, not *radi-o; across*, not *a-cross*.
6. If you are in doubt about the correct division of a word into syllables, consult a standard dictionary.
7. Do not write two words as one. These are written separately: *all right, parcel post, post office*. Your dictionary is the best guide.

SPELLING

576 **Homonyms.** Be careful not to confuse the spelling of the familiar homonyms (words pronounced alike but differing in meaning). (**Heteronyms** are words spelled the same but pronounced differently, as *lead*—to conduct, *lead*—a metal.)

Here are homonyms which everyone should be able to spell and define correctly:

aisle—isle	dew—due	lie—lye
all—awl	die—dye	load—lode
altar—alter	done—dun	loan—lone
ant—aunt	earn—urn	made—maid
arc—ark	fair—fare	mail—male
ascent—assent	faint—feint	main—mane
ate—eight	fain—feign	manner—manor
aught—ought	feat—feet	mantel—mantle
bail—bale	fir—fur	meat—meet
bait—bate	flea—flee	medal—meddle
ball—bawl	flew—flue	might—mite
bare—bear	flour—flower	miner—minor
base—bass	fore—four	moan—mown
be—bee	foul—fowl	muscle—mussel
beach—beech	freeze—frieze	night—knight
beat—beet	gait—gate	none—nun
beau—bow	great—grate	one—won
been—bin	groan—grown	pail—pale
bell—belle	guest—guessed	pain—pane
berth—birth	hair—hare	pause—paws
bier—beer	hall—haul	pair—pare—pear
blew—blue	hale—hail	peace—piece
board—bored	hart—heart	peal—peel
born—borne	heal—heel	plain—plane
bough—bow	hear—here	pore—pour
brake—break	heard—herd	pray—prey
buy—by	heir—air	pride—pried
calendar—calender	hew—hue	principal—principle
canvas—canvass	hoes—hose	profit—prophet
capital—capitol	hole—whole	rain—rein—reign
ceiling—sealing	holy—wholly	raise—raze
cell—sell	hour—our	read—reed
cellar—seller	idol—idle	read—red
cent—sent—scent	in—inn	real—reel
cereal—serial	jam—jamb	rest—wrest
choir—quire	kernel—colonel	rhyme—rime
chord—cord	knead—need	right—write—wright—rite
clause—claws	knew—new	ring—wring
coarse—course	knot—not	road—rode—rowed
council—counsel	know—no	role—roll
creak—creek	lain—lane	rose—rows
currant—current	lead—led	rough—ruff
dear—deer	lessen—lesson	rye—wry

sail—sale	some—sum	to—too—two
scene—seen	son—sun	toe—tow
sea—see	stake—steak	vail—veil—vale
seam—seem	stair—stare	vain—vane—vein
seine—sane	stationary—stationery	vice—vise
sent—scent—cent	staid—stayed	wade—weighed
sew—sow—so	steal—steel	waist—waste
shone—shown	stile—style	wait—weight
sight—site—cite	straight—strait	ware—wear
slay—sleigh	suite—sweet	wave—waive
sleight—slight	tail—tale	way—weigh
slew—slue—slough	their—there	week—weak
soar—sore	throne—thrown	whole—hole
sole—soul	threw—through	wood—would

Spelling List

576A   Every word in the following list of 742 words is rated as of high frequency and usefulness, both for students and adults. The list has been carefully checked with those of many authorities, especially the following:

Ayer, Fred C. "Multiple List of High School Spelling Demons," *A study of High School Spelling Vocabulary*. Austin: The Steck Company.

Fitzgerald, James A. *A Basic Life Spelling Vocabulary*. Milwaukee: The Bruce Publishing Company.

Furness, Edna L. and Boyd, Gertrude A. "231 Real Spelling Demons for High School Students," *The English Journal*, May 1958, 267-270.

Jones, W. Franklin. "One Hundred Spelling Demons of the English Language," *Concrete Investigation of the Material of English Spelling*. Vermillion, S. Dakota: University of South Dakota, 24.

New York City Board of Education. *A Manual to Guide Experimentation with Spelling Lists. A, B, and C*. New York City: Board of Education of the City of New York.

Pollock, T. C., "Spelling Report," *College English*, November 1954, 102-109.

Rinsland, Henry D. *A Basic Vocabulary of Elementary School Children*. New York: Macmillan Company.

ability
absence
absolutely
abundance
accept
acceptance
accident
accidentally
accommodate
accompany
accomplish
accordance
account
accurate
ache
achievement
acknowledge
acquaintance
acquire
across
actual
additional
address
advertisement
advertising
advice
advise
aerial
aeronautics
affect
affectionate
against
aggravate
agressive
agreement
agriculture
alcohol
allowance
all right
already
although
altogether
aluminum
always
amateur
American
among

amount
amusement
analysis
analyze
ancient
angle
anniversary
announce
annual
answer
antenna
anticipate
anxiety
anxious
apologize
apparatus
apparently
appeal
appearance
appetite
application
appoint
appreciate
approach
appropriate
approval
arctic
arguing
argument
arrangement
article
artificial
ascend
ascertain
assignment
assistance
association
assume
assurance
astronaut
athletic
attach
attack
attempt
attendance
attention
attitude

attorney
attractive
audience
authority
automobile
autumn
auxiliary
available
average
aviation
awful
awkward
bachelor
baggage
balance
ballistics
ballot
bandage
banquet
bargain
barrel
basement
basis
become
beggar
beginning
behavior
belief
believe
beneficial
benefited
bicycle
biscuit
blizzard
bookkeeping
bought
boundary
breadth
breathe
brief
brilliant
Britain
broad
bruise
budget
built
bulletin

bureau
burglar
bury
business
busy
cabin
cafeteria
campaign
cancel
candidate
canoe
capacity
captain
career
careless
carriage
carrying
cashier
category
caught
caution
celebration
cemetery
century
certain
certificate
changeable
character
chauffeur
chemistry
chief
chocolate
choice
choose
chose
Christian
circular
civilization
climate
climb
clothes
coach
collar
college
color
column
coming

commence
commercial
commission
committee
communicate
community
comparative
compel
competent
competition
complain
complement
complexion
compliment
computer
conceive
concerning
concert
concession
conclude
concrete
condemn
condition
conference
confidence
congratulate
conscience
conscientious
consequence
considerably
consistent
constitution
continually
continue
controlled
convenience
controversial
convince
co-operate
cordial
corporation
correspondence
cough
could
couldn't
courage
courteous

courtesy
cousin
criticism
cruel
curiosity
curtain
custom
customary
cylinder
daily
deceive
decided
decision
declaration
decorate
defense
definite
definition
delicious
depot
descend
describe
description
desert
deserve
design
desirous
desperate
dessert
determine
develop
development
diamond
dictionary
difference
different
difficulty
diphtheria
diploma
director
disagreeable
disappear
disappoint
disapprove
disastrous
discipline
discover

discuss
disease
distinguish
distribute
divide
divine
division
doctor
dominant
doubt
duly
duplicate
during
dyeing
dying
earnest
easy
economical
economy
ecstasy
effect
efficiency
eighth
either
elaborate
electricity
electronics
elephant
elevator
eligible
embarrass
emergency
emphasize
employment
encourage
endeavor
engineer
English
enormous
enough
entertain
enthusiastic
entrance
envelope
environment
equipment
equipped

especially
essential
establish
evidence
exaggerated
exceed
excellent
except
excite
executive
exercise
exhibition
existence
expedition
expensive
experience
explain
explanation
expression
exquisite
extension
extinct
extremely
fallacy
familiar
famous
fascinate
fashion
fatigue
faucet
favorite
feature
February
federal
fertile
field
fierce
fiery
finally
financially
flight
foreign
fortunate
forty
fountain
fourth
freight

friend	hungry	island	machine
fundamental	hydrogen	issue	magazine
fulfill	hymn	janitor	magnificent
garage	hypocrisy	jealous	maintain
gasoline	idea	jewelry	maintenance
generally	ignorance	journal	majority
generous	illustrate	journey	management
genius	imagination	judgment	manufacture
genuine	imitation	juicy	marriage
geography	immediately	justice	material
glorious	immense	kitchen	mathematics
government	immortal	knowledge	mayor
governor	impatient	label	meant
gracious	importance	laboratory	measure
graduation	impossible	laid	medicine
grammar	improvement	language	medium
grateful	incidentally	laugh	merit
gratitude	inconvenience	laundry	message
grease	independent	lawyer	metal
grief	individual	league	mileage
grievous	industrial	lecture	minimum
grocery	industrious	legal	minute
guarantee	inferior	legislature	missile
guard	influencial	leisurely	mirror
guardian	ingenious	length	mischief
guide	ingenuous	lettuce	mischievous
guilty	inimitable	liability	miserable
gymnasium	innocent	liable	misery
hammer	instance	library	missionary
handkerchief	instead	lieutenant	misspell
handle	institute	license	moisture
handsome	insurance	lightning	monument
happen	intelligence	likely	moral
happiness	interesting	liquid	morale
harbor	interfere	liquor	mortgage
hastily	interpretation	listen	murmur
height	interrupt	literary	musician
heretofore	interview	literature	naturally
heroes	intimate	liveliest	necessary
hesitate	invalid	living	necessity
history	investigate	loneliness	nickel
hoarse	invitation	loose	niece
holiday	invoice	lose	nineteen
honor	it's	losing	ninety
horrible	its	lovable	noticeable
hospital	irresistible	lovely	nuclear
humorous	irrigate	luncheon	nuisance

occasion	procedure	sergeant	touch
occurred	proceed	several	tragedy
occurrence	professor	shining	transferred
omitted	pronunciation	siege	transistor
operate	psychology	similar	treasurer
opinion	pursue	since	tried
opportunity	quaking	sincerely	true
opposite	quiet	solemn	truly
optimism	quite	sophomore	typical
original	radar	spaceship	unanimous
oxygen	radiation	specific	university
paid	realize	specimen	unnecessary
pamphlet	really	speech	upper
paragraph	receipt	sphere	used
parallel	receive	straight	useful
paralyze	received	studying	usually
parliament	recognition	subtle	vacation
particular	recognize	succeed	valuable
pastime	recommend	success	variety
peculiar	reference	sufficient	various
performance	referred	sugar	vegetable
perhaps	relieve	summary	velocity
permanent	religious	superintendent	vengeance
persistent	repetition	suppose	vicinity
personal	representative	suppress	view
personnel	respectfully	surprise	villain
persuade	restaurant	tariff	visible
philosophy	rheumatism	tear	visitor
physician	rhythm	technique	voice
physicist	ridiculous	telegram	volume
planned	roommate	temperature	wander
plastics	sacrifice	temporary	warrant
pleasant	sacrilegious	terrible	weather
pneumonia	said	territory	weird
possession	salary	theater	whether
practical	sandwich	therefore	whom
precede	satellite	they	whose
precious	satire	they're	width
preference	satisfactory	thief	woman
prejudice	schedule	thoroughly	women
prepare	science	though	worst
prevalent	scissors	tired	wouldn't
prisoner	secretary	tobacco	writing
privilege	seize	together	written
probably	separate	tongue	yield

VOCABULARY BUILDING

577 Vocabulary. One's ability to express his own thoughts and to understand the expression of the thoughts of others is measured by his knowledge of the meaning of words. A good vocabulary is, therefore, a valuable aid to success in any field, and must include the vocabularies of the student's special fields of interest, with their **synonyms** (words of the same general meaning but different in their specific application) and **antonyms** (words of opposite meaning).

577A Dictionary Use. The use of a standard unabridged dictionary is valuable in building a vocabulary. It gives extensive information about every word—its pronunciation, part of speech (36), derivation, standing as to usage, various meanings, synonyms, and antonyms. In a section usually at the front of the dictionary, all symbols of pronunciation are explained and the diacritical marks are fully illustrated.

577B Plan for Vocabulary. The building of a vocabulary requires time, patience, and persistence. One good plan is for one to write in a notebook all unfamiliar words which he reads or hears. Unfamiliar words found in reading one's own books should be marked so that the meaning may be studied in the context.

577C Vocabulary and Verse. Through the writing of rhymed verse (526A-526E), one may enlarge his vocabulary, because words must be selected for meaning as well as for sound. The sonnet (526K, 526L) is a good stanza form to use because of its rigid rhyme requirements. The limerick (526N) is also a good form which may be used in either light or serious mood. Writing parodies (imitations) of popular verse is not only fun but a profitable exercise in word substitution. Specimens of these types of writing are to be found in current newspapers and magazines. The improvised limerick and sonnet below suggest possibilities:

SUCCESS

You think you are well on your way,
Assured you make progress each day;
Yet, nevertheless,
Your final success
Depends on the words that you say.

WORDS

The words we use may be but stumbling blocks
To make more arduous our upward way—
Along our path but rough, projecting rocks
To bruise our weary feet from day to day;
And yet, it's folly we are thus oppressed,
For words may help us on to higher things:
One who with mastery of words is blest
Not only upward toils, but starward goes on wings.
Unwise are they who fail to count the cost
Of clumsy, careless words that flout success,
But wisdom theirs who see as won or lost
Through use of words life's greatest happiness.
He who for artistry in language strives
Finds rich return: with *words* we shape our lives.

578 Library. Nearly all libraries are now using the Dewey Decimal System, which classifies all works exclusive of fiction into ten groups. Following is a simple description:

000-099	General works, such as encyclopedias
100-199	Philosophy, psychology
200-299	Religion, mythology
300-399	Social sciences, such as government and economics, and books on clubs, holidays, and etiquette
400-499	Grammar and study of languages
500-599	Natural sciences: mathematics, physics, chemistry, animals, insects, birds
600-699	Useful arts: inventions, gardening, cooking, sewing, aeronautics, engineering, medicine, agriculture
700-799	Fine arts, such as drawing and music
800-899	Literature (except fiction)
900-999	History, travel, geography, biography

Certain books may not be shelved according to their class number.

1. Short-story collections may be marked *SC* and shelved separately. They are arranged alphabetically by the last name of the editor.
2. Books of biography are shelved according to the last name of the person they are about. Some libraries use the Dewey Decimal number 921, many prefer 92, and some use only the letter *B* to indicate biography. Below either 921, 92, or *B* is the initial of the person written about.
3. Reference books like encyclopedias and atlases are usually shelved together. The letter *R* above the number indicates a reference book.

Eight: STRUCTURAL AND TRANSFORMATIONAL GRAMMAR

STRUCTURAL LINGUISTICS

579 **Structural linguistics** is a valuable method of studying languages, especially a variety of languages, to determine how their structure contributes to the meaning of their words. It is perhaps particularly useful in studying the anything-but-primitive languages of primitive peoples and in the description of any spoken language, since it may indicate sounds, voice inflections, pauses, and so on   (599-604).*

580   The **traditional terminology** of English grammar has had to be reinterpreted in modern times to apply more accurately to English. It is based on terminology that originally applied to Latin, and English does not fit readily into a Latin mold. In the same way, the terminology that has been adapted to English must be further adapted if it is to fit other, quite different languages. Our "parts of speech," for example, are not the same as Navajo "parts of speech." Some languages have categories wholly lacking in English—forms for "things in sight," "things not in sight," for example. For this reason a study of language based on structure—divorced as far as possible from the meaning of ordinary grammatical terminology—avoids some of the confusions and misconceptions that arise when terminology designed for one language is used for another.

581   Structural linguistics also offers valuable insights into our language to those who are thoroughly trained in traditional grammar. Those who undertake any advanced study of English should expect to become familiar with the terminology and approach of this relatively new method of language study.

582   **Objectives of Grammar Study.** It should be kept in mind while studying a new approach to the explanation of a language that the language itself is not changed because the description of it changes: the problems remain the same. Whatever system one studies, it should be one that can be applied to the problems of writing and speaking with clarity, with effectiveness, and with a minimum of irrelevant and unintended social friction. The problems of usage remain the same whatever the system of grammar, and (although there is room for difference of opinion) substantially the same answers should be given to such questions as those concerning agreement of verbs, agreement of pronouns, the use of the subjunctive, the formation of

* *Numbers in parentheses refer to sections of this book.*

plurals, capitalization, punctuation, and the other mechanics of writing. In other words, the rules may be reformulated but not changed (except as usage changes), because the rules must reflect the usage of the society rather than the predilections of the grammarians. The objectives also should remain the practical ones of making more effective the use and comprehension of language.

583 The **definitions** of structural linguistics are quite different from those of traditional grammar. No definitions yet developed are entirely free of ambiguities and unexplained terms. The structural linguist tries to avoid the problems of traditional definitions by defining his terms by means of structural examples and formal characteristics. To be complete, such definitions must involve so many formulas as to be unwieldy. But, as with traditional definitions, sufficiently clear ideas can be given to permit further development by the use of additional examples and analogies. The following explanations are intended merely to give some idea of the approach used by some widely studied linguists. Since no two structural linguists use quite the same terminology and definitions, those given here certainly cannot be final or complete. This description is based primarily on the work of those who have tried to adapt the subject to undergraduate college students and even to high-school students, and it should be understood to be only a partial description of the technique employed.

584 The **parts of speech** in structural linguistics parallel in many ways those of traditional grammar, but there are important differences, as will be seen below. For this reason some linguists prefer to avoid traditional terms altogether, but since this introduction is intended for those already grounded in traditional terminology, it is obvious that parallels should be drawn and differences brought out. Many linguists use the traditional terms **nouns** and **pronouns, verbs, adjectives,** and **adverbs** for the important form classes, and these terms are used in this chapter.

Form Classes

585 The form class **nouns and pronouns** is illustrated by the italicized words as used in the patterns below:

The *boy* is honest.
The *boys* are honest.
The *boys* saw *him.*
He saw the *boys.*
They ate the *peaches.*

Words that fit into sentence positions structurally similar to those shown above are nouns or pronouns. These are not substitution patterns: you do not say "The *desk* is honest," "They ate the *courage*." But *desk* and *courage* are nouns. One must learn to realize what patterns of words are structurally similar. The position of a word in a sentence helps to classify it, but one must understand sentence structure before he can analyze words in this way. This applies to the study of all of the form classes.

586 One must also remember that a large proportion of English words may be used as more than one part of speech (50). A toy boat may *sink* (verb) in a *sink* (noun). You may fall *down* (adverb) and not make a first *down* (noun) in a football game. One can determine the class of a word only when it is used in a sentence, but other tests may also be needed to determine the class of a word in a sentence (see 589).

587 Nouns and pronouns generally show **singular and plural number.** Those in this form class that correspond to nouns (51-58) usually add *s* to show the plural (see 73-89). Those that correspond to pronouns (123) show number by entirely different words: *he (she)—they*. But the determiners (598) *this* and *that* also have the plural forms *these* and *those*. Verbs (590) indicate a singular meaning in the third person present tense by adding *s*: He *runs;* they *run.*

588 Another **formal characteristic** of nouns—not pronouns—is that they may have another *s* ending, in writing marked by an apostrophe, to show possession or some such relationship (see 111-121). There are exceptions as explained in 11C-117. Other characteristics of this class are that nouns and pronouns may be "marked" (or modified) by determiners (598) or adjectives (592) that are not in noun positions. Nouns and pronouns may also be "marked" in a different way (not modified) by prepositions (598). Nouns also correlate in many ways with pronouns. There are other characteristics that mark words of this form class, but these will illustrate what is meant by the formal and structural approach.

589 Most nouns may be used to modify other nouns. For instance in the sentence "He planted a rose bush" *rose* is a noun, not an adjective (592), because it cannot be modified by an intensive (598), and so on, as adjectives are, and it cannot appear in other adjective positions. You cannot say "it is a very rose bush" or "The bush is rose." (On the same basis "traditional" grammarians have sometimes argued that nouns may modify nouns.)

590 The form class **verbs** is illustrated by the italicized words as used in the following patterns:

They *see* the fire.

He *came* alone.

Most verbs show a few changes in form that are associated with tense (185), person (66), and number (see 165-208). Most of them regularly form definite patterns with auxiliaries (598), such as *may, is, was, had, have, should.* They usually have a form ending in *-ing* (attached to a basic form). It is quite common to treat the word *be* (*be, am, is, are, was, were, been, being*) as having a separate class of its own, and not as a verb. But it may also be an auxiliary.

591   Verbs may modify nouns: *singing* teakettle, *running* brook, *treated* leather. But some *-ing* and *-ed* words are adjectives (592)—those for instance, that form a pattern with *very: interesting* person (He is *very interesting*). Also some *-ing* words may take noun positions: "His *writing* is very poor." compare 195-196.)

592   The form class **adjectives** is illustrated by the italicized words as used in the following patterns:

The boy was *good.*

The *slender* girl came in.

The very *efficient* secretary resigned.

Most adjectives have forms that show comparison (286).

593   **Adverbs** are illustrated by the italicized words as used in the following patterns:

She sang *beautifully.*

He *often* fails to meet the payments.

The dog jumped *up.*

Most adverbs also show comparison (318).

594   **The form classes** must be recognized if one is to understand a sentence; otherwise the sentence is ambiguous. The form of a word, as well as its position in the sentence, often indicates its form class. For instance, many nouns end in *-tion, -ness (relation, goodness);* many verbs end in *-ing, -ed (bringing, acted),* but these endings sometimes mark adjectives (591); many adjectives end in *-like, -ful, -less, -ish, -ous (childlike, graceful, fruitless, bookish, famous);* and many (not all) adverbs end in *-ly (prettily, slowly);* but some adjectives also end in *-ly (lovely, ugly, homely).*

595   While **formal characteristics** of words are of help in determining the form class to which a word belongs, they cannot be relied on fully. Distinctive forms are rare in English, and formal characteristics may sometimes be completely at variance with structural considerations. For example, in the sentence "The richest lived on the north shore," the word *richest* has a formal characteristic of an adjective: the ending *-est.* It may also be modified, as are adjectives, by an intensive: the *very richest.* On the other hand, it is marked by *the* as a noun, it is tied like a noun to a verb, and it can otherwise be substituted for nouns in noun positions. Frequently the view is taken that the position supersedes the form of the word and that therefore *richest* is a noun in the sentence given (compare 307).

Structure Words

596 Structure words require a large number of groups to be clearly distinguished. These words have little meaning of their own, but they contribute significantly to the structural meaning of sentences. Every linguist uses a different grouping of words so that all that can be done here is to illustrate the approach used by certain widely known linguists.

597 Structure-word groups include all words that are not included in the four form classes. They will of course include words traditionally called **prepositions, conjunctions,** and **interjections.** But they also include some words traditionally called **adjectives, adverbs,** and **verbs.** These groups include only a small number of English words— a few hundred. The form classes, of course, include hundreds of thousands of words.

598 An illustrative classification of structure-word groups:

Determiners: *a, an, the,* and sometimes *some, these, each,* and so on. These mark nouns.

Auxiliaries: *am, are, is, (be), may, will, should,* and so on, when used with verbs. (The word *be* may also be a special form of verb.) Auxiliaries are verb markers.

Prepositions: *with, at, on, under,* and so on. These combine in patterns with nouns and pronouns.

Intensives: words that generally lend emphasis to adjectives or adverbs (sometimes also to verbs): **very, really, rather, too,** and so on. Unlike adverbs, some of these do not pattern with verbs—one does not say, "He plays *very.*"

Coordinators: *and, but, or, nor, for,* etc. Only coordinating conjunctions are included. The sentence connectors, such as *therefore, however, nevertheless,* may be given a different designation.

Subordinators: words like *because, since, after* (subordinating conjunctions) that join sentence groups into larger structures. Words like *who, what, which* (relatives) are sometimes classified with this group, sometimes in a separate group.

Question markers: *who, where, what, which, how, why,* etc., when they signal a question.

There are a few words like *yes, no, not, please, hello, good-by, oh,* and so on. To be accurately classified, these few words would require a large number of group designations.

Phonemes

599 Our speech is made up of a number of distinctive sound groups, or phonemes, that may be represented by symbols. Each phoneme has variations depending on its phonetic environment, but it is recognized by a native speaker as essentially the same sound wherever it occurs in his language. For example, sound represented by *t* in English is not the same in each of the following words: *tone, stove, trip, butter, butler, eighth;* but it is the same phoneme. Phonemic transcription is enclosed in diagonal lines: /t/. Stress, pitch, and juncture are also phonemes (601-604). An understanding of phonemes is requisite to the thorough study of foreign languages and of our own spoken language.

Morphemes

600 Any voice signal, phoneme, or group of phonemes that contributes to meaning and that recurs with relatively constant meaning in different contexts is a morpheme; it must not be further divisible into smaller meaningful elements. The word *girlish* is composed of the two morphemes *girl* and *-ish;* neither can be divided into smaller units which recur with the same meaning; they both occur in other contexts with relatively the same meanings; that is, the morpheme *girl* has the same meaning in *girls* as it does in *girlish,* and the morpheme *-ish* has the same meaning in *boyish* as it has in *girlish.*

Intonation

601 In speaking we use stress, pitch, and juncture to add meaning to words. Taken together, these are intonation. Intonation sometimes determines the form class of words and therefore must be taken into account by a writer. A sentence that may suggest the wrong intonation may be ambiguous; unless punctuation will make it clear, it should be rewritten. Such sentences are rare. But an understanding of the meanings contributed by intonation are important in studying speech. Note the changes in meaning given by shifting the emphasis in the following sentence:

> *Why* don't you sing?
> Why *don't* you sing?
> Why don't *you* sing?
> Why don't you *sing?*

602 **Stress.** Four degrees of stress (loudness) are usually identified in English. The stress symbols, from softest to loudest, are /˘/ˋ/ˆ/ˊ/. A sentence may be marked as follows: *Thĕ rédbùd hăd ă rêd búd.* Stress contributes strongly to meaning, as in differentiating *redbud* and *red bud.*

603 **Pitch.** Four levels of pitch are distinguished, marked as follows from lowest to highest: /1/2/3/4/. Pitch may also be marked for a sentence by lines above and below letters, the higher the line, the higher the pitch. The following shows both ways of marking pitch, a feeling of exasperation giving a high pitch to *are:*

> 2   4 2   3. 1
>
> Where are you going?

> Where | are | you | go | ing?

As an ordinary question this sentence might be marked for pitch as follows:

> Where are you | go | ing?

604 **Juncture.** There are four junctures: plus juncture /+/, single-bar juncture /|/, double-bar juncture /||/, and double-cross juncture /#/.

Plus juncture is the suggestion of a break between phonemes that distinguishes, for instance, between *ice+cream* and *I+scream.* Actually, although the same phonemes are used, there is a slight difference in them. There is usually no actual break or pause in the sound.

Single-bar juncture occurs after a primary (loudest) stress in a sentence if the pitch remains the same: *The girl in the car | is my cousin.*

Double-bar juncture occurs after a primary stress when there is a slight rise in pitch: *Major Hamilton || flying a routine mission || made a remarkable discovery.* This juncture corresponds roughly to points in a sentence that would be punctuated by commas, or possibly dashes; but the correspondence is not exact. It may also occur at the end of certain questions.

Double-cross juncture occurs when the pitch falls and the voice trails into silence: *We lived there ten years # however || I didn't like it #.* This juncture frequently corresponds to end punctuation, especially the period, or to the semicolon; but the correspondence is not exact.

605 This brief outline of structural linguistics will of course raise many questions that cannot be answered here. One should not assume, however, that such questions cannot be answered. Although much work remains to be done in the field, a great many problems have been thoroughly and satisfactorily worked out. A study of the subject can be highly rewarding, and many of the books listed in the Bibliography at the end of this chapter will be of special value for those interested in the study of linguistics. Most of these books assume a thorough knowledge of conventional grammar.

TRANSFORMATIONAL GRAMMAR

606   The basic assumption of this significant new grammar of the linguists is that all the sentences in a language can be derived from "kernel" sentences by means of transformations. This grammar may also be defined as a method for "generating" the sentences of a language, so that you will find the term generative grammar as well as transformational grammar applied to the systems of language study based on the assumptions implicit in the idea of deriving complex sentence structures from the simplest possible patterns.

Kernel Sentences

607   The basic or kernel sentences of a language are simple declarative sentences with verbs in the active voice. Theoretically, a native speaker of the language will recognize these sentences as grammatically correct, so that more complicated sentences derived from them by strict transformation rules will also be grammatically correct. Negative, passive, and interrogative sentences are all produced by transformation of kernel sentences. So also are sentences with most kinds of adjective and adverbial modifiers, or conjunctions or other connectives. These, of course, include the most sophisticated sentences of the language.

Simple Transformations

608   Teachers of English are already familiar with the ways in which an active sentence, for example, may be changed to a passive. The active sentence must have an object:

He shot a *tiger*.

In the passive, the object becomes the subject:

A *tiger* was shot by him.

The phrase *by him* replaces the subject *he* of the active sentence, but it is now not grammatically necessary:

A tiger was shot.

The description of the language is simplified by being limited basically to a small number of simple sentences of this kind. The transformations that generate all other sentences from these kernel sentences are numerous and varied, but each follows invariable steps, and it is this constancy of the transformations that gives the greatest promise to the generative method.

The Basic Sentence Patterns

609 It will at once be seen that the basic pattern of the kernel sentences is the familiar subject-predicate structure.

	Subject	Predicate
Pattern I:	Boys	fight.
Pattern II:	Boys	play ball.
Pattern III A:	Boys	become men.
Pattern III B:	Boys	are fighters.
Pattern IV A:	Boys	seem brave.
Pattern IV B:	Boys	are brave.
Pattern V:	Boys	are everywhere.

610 PATTERN I

Pattern I, the simplest pattern, may consist of only a noun and a verb—**NV**: *Boys argue*. But the noun is often preceded by a noun-determiner: a structure word (596) such as *a, an,* or *the*. The symbol for noun-determiner may be written **(n-d)**, the parentheses indicating that the determiner is not always necessary. Every basic pattern has a subject that may be written as **(n-d) + N**. But the predicates are different for each pattern: they are what distinguish the patterns.

The following are samples of Pattern I sentences:

(n-d)	N	V
	Boys	argue.
The	corn	grows.
	Bees	buzz.

611 PATTERN II

Many verbs require complements and therefore will not fit into Pattern I. All the other patterns include complements, which may be nouns, adjectives, or adverbs. Patterns II and III will require noun complements. These are Pattern II sentences:

(n-d) N^1	V	(n-d) N^2
The boys	played	football.
Jane	likes	music.
Columbus	discovered	America.

The **direct object** is labeled N^2 because it does not indicate the same thing as the subject noun, N^1.

Some verbs can be used in either Pattern I or Pattern II. You can say either "The boys played" or "The boys played baseball." Pattern I verbs are used as **intransitives,** and Pattern II verbs as **transitives** (169-171).

612   PATTERN III

There are always two nouns in Pattern III linked by verbs such as *become* or *remain* (III A) or forms of *be* (III B). *Be* is different from other words in many ways and therefore sentences with forms of *be* are grouped separately in each pattern.

The symbol for a predicate is **VP** and the symbol for "is rewritten as" is an arrow:→. The predicate for Pattern III A is written as **VP → V + N¹**: Thus there are two positions (or "slots") in this pattern labeled **N¹**, because both nouns refer to the same person or thing.

613   PATTERN III A

(n-d)N¹	V	(n-d)N¹
Boys	become	men.
Jim	became	a salesman.
The team	became	champions.
Joe	remained	a bore.

614   PATTERN III B

VP → be + N¹

(n-d)N¹	be	(n-d)N¹
Churchill	was	a statesman.
Whales	are	mammals.
Fred	is	a halfback.

615   PATTERN IV

The first three sentence patterns require only two form classes: noun and verb. Pattern IV requires an adjective. The verbs used most often in Pattern IV A are *seem, taste, look, feel, smell, sound, appear, grow, get,* as well as *become* and *remain.*

616   PATTERN IV A

VP → V + Adj

(n-d)N	V	Adj
The boys	got	angry.
The sun	grew	hot.
The fruit	tastes	good.
The fur	feels	soft.

617 PATTERN IV B

Some form of *be* appears in this pattern. **VP → be + Adj.**

(n-d) N	be	Adj
The eggs	were	fresh.
The heat	was	uncomfortable.
The men	are	brave.

618 PATTERN V

This pattern is unusual but important. **VP → be + Adv.** The adverbs in this pattern are usually place adverbs, but occasionally adverbs of time.

(n-d)N	be	Adv
The guests	are	outside.
Water	is	everywhere.
The meeting	is	tomorrow.
The planes	were	above.

619 The kernel sentences of transformational grammar may seem completely familiar to you. It is, of course, intended that they should. In this grammar you start with what you already know and largely understand. From these simple basic sentences you can, with strict transformation rules, generate entirely new sentences—as long and as complicated as you wish. And if your kernel sentences are grammatically correct, your transformations will be grammatically correct.

Transformations

620 Scholars who have tried to write complete descriptions of a language have found that a dozen tightly packed volumes were not enough. A language has an almost unlimited diversity of structures. But quite ordinary persons learn to use their native language in childhood and often to use it with considerable skill. Essentially, it seems, a language structure is not as complicated as it appears to be. Transformational grammar tries to find the fundamental simplicity of a language in a small set of kernel sentences. The transformation rules give us all the rest of the language.

The There Transformation

621 A common type of English sentence begins with the expletive *there* (232):

There is a messenger here.

This of course is a transformation. From what pattern is this sentence derived? You can easily find out by rewording the sentence without *there:*

A messenger is here.

You can see at once that this is a Pattern V sentence. What happens in the transformation? Primarily, the verb is put before the subject, a reversal of the characteristic English word order. Is the form of *be* changed in this reversal? Does *there* have number? No, as used here, the word *there* is merely a signal that the normal subject-Predicate order of English is being reversed—it is a meaningless word otherwise. (Do not confuse the expletive *there* with the adverb *there* indicating place). The word *is* continues to agree in person and number with its subject *messenger.*

622   In general the *there* transformation can be derived only from Pattern V. However, if the predicate is expanded by using the auxiliary *be,* a transformation originating with Pattern I may sometimes be obtained.

Several messengers *leave.*

Several messengers *are leaving.*

There *are* several messengers *leaving.*

This is an illustration of the way in which specific restrictions must often be placed on a transformation process.

Transformations Requiring Auxiliaries

623   The final *there* transformation illustrates an important characteristic of English word order. Several transformations introduce a reversal into the normal subject-predicate order. If an auxiliary has been introduced into the predicate, only the auxiliary may be placed before the subject (this applies also to a combination of auxiliaries such as *may have been*). Often an auxiliary expansion is obligatory, as in the *there* transformation based on Pattern V.

The Question Transformations

624   If an ordinary auxiliary *(can, may, shall, will, must, have, be)* or auxiliary combination has first been used to expand the predicate, the question transformation may be carried out as with *there* and auxiliaries. However, only the first auxiliary is moved in front of the subject, the main part of the verb following the subject:

Mr. Baron has arrived.   →   Has Mr. Baron arrived?

Herbert is skating.   →   Is Herbert skating?

Herbert might have been skating.   →   Might Herbert have been skating?

But if no regular auxiliary is present, the main verb usually cannot be placed before the subject (although in older English such constructions were possible). We cannot change *Herbert skates* to *Skates Herbert?* In this situation we use the special word *do* to fill the need:

Does Herbert skate?

Exceptions to the requirement of an auxiliary for the question transformation are *be* and sometimes *have* when used as main verbs.

He has enough. → Has he enough?
It is ready. → Is it ready?

But in sentences such as "He has it," American English, unlike British English, requires *do* for the question transformation:

Does he have it? *Not* Has he it?

The word *do* may also be a main verb, but it also requires the auxiliary *do* for this transformation.

Did he do the work?

The same type of transformation may be used with some questions introduced by the question markers (598) such as *when, where, why:*

Jane has left. → Why has Jane left?
She will come back. → When will she come back?
Fred lives here. → Where does Fred live?

There are other types of questions, but they need not be treated here.

The Negative Transformation

625 The negative transformation also requires an auxiliary, but the word order is not changed. Add *not* (or *n't*) to the auxiliary or the first word of an auxiliary combination. *Be* and sometimes *have* are exceptions in this transformation also.

She will come back. → She won't come back.
Fred lives here. → Fred doesn't live here.
She is here. → She isn't here.

The necessity for *do* if no other auxiliary is present is the same as for a question transformation.

The Passive Transformation

626 Anyone can see the difference between the sentence "The woman became an actress" and "The woman read the play." One can also see that the second sentence can be transformed into the passive, but the first one cannot. We cannot say "The actress was become by the woman," but we can say "The play was read by the woman." Pattern

IIIA sentences cannot be transformed into the passive voice, but Pattern II sentences can be.

Modification Transformations

627 "The woman is intelligent" is a basic sentence Pattern IVB, and "The woman screamed" is a Pattern I sentence. "The intelligent woman screamed" is not a basic sentence but a transformation. It may be derived from the first two kernel sentences:

The woman is intelligent. ⎫

                    ⎬ The intelligent woman screamed.

The woman screamed. ⎭

Complex Sentence Transformations

628 There is nothing difficult even in deriving a complex sentence with an adjective clause from simple kernel sentences. The relative clause is derived from a kernel sentence called the *consumer:*

SOURCE: It seems valuable. (IVA)
CONSUMER: I found a document. (II)
RESULT: I found a document that seems valuable.

SOURCE: I bought a watch. (II)
CONSUMER: The watch was an heirloom. (IIIB)
RESULT: The watch which I bought was an heirloom.

629 The transformations illustrated here are simplified examples of the transformational method. None of the transformational rules are given because to talk clearly about them requires the use of symbols in precise ways. The symbols look very complicated at first, but they greatly simplify the presentation and use of the method. A full explanation is impossible of course in this space, but it is hoped that some of the underlying simplicity and power of the transformational method has been suggested.

BIBLIOGRAPHY

General Works on English Grammar and Usage

630 CURME, GEORGE O., *A Grammar of the English Language*, Boston: D. C. Heath and Company (Vol. II, *Parts of Speech and Accidence*, and Vol. III, *Syntax*)

EVANS, BERGEN, AND EVANS, CORNELIA, *A Dictionary of Contemporary American Usage*, New York: Random House

FRIES, CHARLES CARPENTER, *American English Grammar*, New York: D. Appleton-Century Company

HORWILL, H. W., *A Dictionary of Modern American Usage*, Second Edition, London: Oxford University Press

HOUSE, HOMER C., AND HARMAN, SUSAN E., *Descriptive English Grammar*, Second Edition, Englewood Cliffs, New Jersey: Prentice-Hall

JESPERSEN, OTTO, *A Modern English Grammar on Historical Principles*, London: George Allen & Unwin, Ltd., 7 vols.

JESPERSEN, OTTO, *Essentials of English Grammar*, New York: Henry Holt and Co., Inc.

MARCKWARDT, ALBERT H., *American English*, New York: Oxford University Press

MATHEWS, MITFORD M., editor, *A Dictionary of Americanisms on Historical Principles*, Chicago: The University of Chicago Press

PARTRIDGE, ERIC, *The Concise Usage and Abusage: A Modern Guide to Good English*, New York: Philosophical Library

POOLEY, ROBERT C., *Teaching English Grammar*, New York: Appleton-Century-Crofts

ROBERTS, PAUL, *Understanding English*, New York: Harper & Brothers

SAPIR, EDWARD, *Language*, New York: Harcourt, Brace and Co. (available in paper binding)

SUMMEY, GEORGE, JR., *American Punctuation*, New York: The Ronald Press Company

171

Works on Structural and Transformational Grammar

631 ALLEN, HAROLD B., editor, *Reading in Applied English Linguistics,* Second Edition, New York: Appleton-Century-Crofts

BLOOMFIELD, LEONARD, *Language,* New York: Henry Holt and Company

CHOMSKY, NOAM, *Syntactic Structures,* 'S-Gravenhage: Mouton & Co.

FRANCIS, W. NELSON, *The Structure of American English,* New York: Ronald Press

FRIES, CHARLES CARPENTER, *The Structure of English,* New York: Harcourt, Brace and Company.

———, "Advances in Linguistics," *College English,* October 1961, pp. 30-37

GLEASON, H. A. JR., *An Introduction to Descriptive Linguistics,* Revised Edition, New York: Holt, Rinehart and Winston

HALL, ROBERT A., JR., *Linguistics and Your Language,* Garden City, New York: Doubleday and Company, Inc.

HARRIS, ZELLIG A., *Structural Linguistics,* Chicago: University of Chicago Press (Phoenix P 52-paperback)

HACKETT, CHARLES F., *A Course in Modern Linguistics,* New York: Macmillan Company

IVES, SUMMER, "Linguistics in the Classroom," *College English,* December 1955, pp. 165-172

LEES, ROBERT B., *The Grammar of English Nominalizations,* Bloomington, Indiana: Research Center in Anthropology, Folklore, and Linguistics

ROBERTS, PAUL, *Patterns of English,* New York: Harcourt, Brace and Company

———, *English Sentences,* New York: Harcourt, Brace and World, Inc.

———, *English Syntax: An Introduction to Transformational Grammar,* New York: Harcourt, Brace and World, Inc.

SLEDD, JAMES, *A Short Introduction to English Grammar,* Chicago: Scott, Foresman and Company

STAGEBERG, NORMAN C. *An Introductory English Grammar,* New York: Holt, Rinehart and Winston

TWADDELL, W. F., *The English Verb Auxiliaries,* Providence Rhode Island: Brown University Press (paperbound)

VIERTEL, JOHN, "Generative Grammars," *College Composition and Communication,* May 1964, pp. 65-81.

INDEX

(Numbers not otherwise designated refer to sections of this book.)